Fulbright Papers

PROCEEDINGS OF COLLOQUIA

SPONSORED BY THE
UNITED STATES–UNITED KINGDOM
EDUCATIONAL COMMISSION:
THE
FULBRIGHT COMMISSION,
LONDON

Volume 5

*Information technology:
the public issues*

The Fulbright Programme of Educational Exchanges, which has been in operation since 1946, aims to promote mutual understanding between the United States of America and other nations. It now operates in more than 120 countries, with forty-three bi-national commissions involved in its administration. In the United Kingdom the Commission aims to offer qualified British and American nationals the opportunity to exchange significant knowledge and educational experience in fields of consequence to the two countries, and thereby to contribute to a deeper mutual understanding of Anglo-American relations and to broaden the means by which the two societies can further their understanding of each other's cultures. Among its activities the Commission promotes annual colloquia on topics of Anglo-American interest; the proceedings are published in this series.

1. *Lexicography: an emerging international profession*
ed. R. Ilson

2. *Ethics and international relations*
ed. Anthony Ellis

3. *Orphan diseases and orphan drugs*
ed. I. Herbert Scheinberg and J. M. Walshe

4. *Regenerating the cities*
The UK crisis and the US experience
ed. Michael Parkinson and Bernard Foley

5. *Information technology: the public issues*
ed. Raymond Plant, Frank Gregory and Alan Brier

Information technology: the public issues

edited by
RAYMOND PLANT,
FRANK GREGORY
and ALAN BRIER

MANCHESTER
UNIVERSITY PRESS
IN ASSOCIATION WITH
THE FULBRIGHT COMMISSION, LONDON

DISTRIBUTED EXCLUSIVELY IN THE USA AND CANADA BY
ST. MARTIN'S PRESS

COPYRIGHT © THE US – UK EDUCATIONAL COMMISSION, 1988

Published by MANCHESTER UNIVERSITY PRESS
Oxford Road, Manchester M13 9PL
and Room 400, 175 Fifth Avenue,
New York, NY 10010, USA

Distributed exclusively in the USA and Canada by St. Martin's Press, Inc., 175 Fifth Avenue, New York, NY 10010, USA

in association with THE FULBRIGHT COMMISSION,
6 Porter Street, London W1M 2HR

British Library cataloguing in publication data
Information technology: the public issues. — (Fulbright papers; v. 5)
1. Technology—Social aspects
2. Information storage and retrieval systems—Social aspects
I. Plant, Raymond   II. Gregory, Frank
III. Brier, Alan   IV. Series
303.4'83   T14.5

Library of Congress cataloging in publication data applied for

ISBN 0-7190-2473-0 *hardback*

Printed in Great Britain
by The Alden Press, Oxford

Contents

Foreword   JOHN E. FRANKLIN   vii

1 Taking control? Some aspects of the relationship between information technology, government policy and democracy   JOHN STREET   1

2 The role of the information society concept in IT policy; some international comparisons and a critique   DAVID LYON   21

3 Internationalisation and the production of technology and information   HOWARD WILLIAMS   43

4 Government regulation and innovation in information technology   DAVID J. GOODMAN   62

5 British industrial policy and the information technology sector   JILL HILLS   79

6 Managers and information technology   J. H. SMITH   95

7 Technological innovation and education — the case of the microcomputer   RAINER RUGE   109

8 Mapping the social sciences: the contribution of technology to information retrieval   EUGENE GARFIELD, ROBERT KIMBERLEY and DAVID A. PENDLEBURY   129

9 Information technology and defence decision-making   MAJOR-GENERAL G. R. OEHLERS   142

10 The relevance of information technology for policing — dilemmas of control and freedom   DAVID J. O'DOWD   148

| 11 | Computing in the human services | BRYAN GLASTONBURY | 164 |
| 12 | Pangloss, Pandora or Jefferson? Three scenarios for the future of technology and democracy | BENJAMIN R. BARBER | 177 |

Notes on contributors 192
Index 194

Foreword

This volume records the proceedings of the Fulbright Colloquium on Information Technology: The Public Issues which was held at the University of Southampton from Tuesday 16 September to Friday 29 September 1986. The Fulbright Commission in London felt that an Anglo–American conference on this subject was particularly appropriate at this time. Information technology (IT) has been at the forefront of informed debate on both sides of the Atlantic for a number of years and has been recognised as an issue of major importance in both countries, affecting all strands of society.

In meeting its aim of promoting Anglo–American cultural understanding, the Commission sponsors at least one, and generally two, colloquia each year on subjects of mutual interest and importance to the USA and the UK. These meetings of distinguished scholars and practitioners in specialist fields augment the Commission's traditional awards of studentships, scholarships and fellowships to British and American citizens for study, teaching, research or work experience in the other's country. Over 10,000 such exchanges have been supported in this way by the Commission since it was established in 1948.

The Colloquium at Southampton touched on a wide range of issues affecting every citizen in his or her contact with government, industry, the armed services, the police and other key organisations in society. The Anglo–American dimension was fully probed by speakers from both countries and the specialist presentations and discussions highlighted many important points of significance for all.

The opinions expressed are, of course, personal to the contributors and do not necessarily reflect the views of the Commission. Nevertheless, the Commission believes that the publication of the Colloquium proceedings will be welcomed by a wide audience. Information technology is critical to the effective working of the modern world and the Fulbright Commission is very pleased that it was able to support the University of Southampton in mounting a Colloquium on this important and highly relevant subject.

JOHN E. FRANKLIN, *Executive Director*
United States–United Kingdom Educational Commission:
The Fulbright Commission, London

Taking control? Some aspects of the relationship between information technology, government policy and democracy

JOHN STREET
University of East Anglia

INTRODUCTION

What are the implications for democracy of the development of information technology (IT)? Concern about the impact of IT on political practices and political ideas is becoming increasingly commonplace. It takes a variety of forms, from revulsion to cautious welcome, to enthusiastic embrace. Four examples serve to suggest some of the more interesting lines of thought:

> Not only is the communications revolution changing the way of traditional political processes, it is beginning to force us to recognise that new political theories need to be devised. [F. Williams (1982), p. 198]

> To preserve democracy in an information-based economy, [political institutions] should be decentralised, flexible and open. [S. Williams (1985), p. 16]

> Although it brings new kinds of risks, modern telecommunications technology can be developed as an instrument for democratic discourse. [Barber (1984), p. 274]

> It is not that we cannot live without computers, but that we will be different people because we live with them. [Bolter (1984), p. 10]

Many other quotations — telling of the computer's threat to privacy, or of the IBM's threat to national sovereignty, or of the promise of a global village — could have served equally well to make the point that IT raises new issues for those concerned with developing a coherent account of the realities of, and possibilities for, democracy.

Although information technology is having a dramatic effect upon the way we live and think, it has been relatively slow in goading political theorists in particular and students of politics generally (with notable exceptions) into action. Compare the response of political scientists to IT with the response of philosophers to genetic engineering and nuclear weapons; see Hardin (1985); Kenny (1985); Glover (1984). Nonetheless, there is now a fast growing body of literature which suggests that there is much for social scientists to consider and contribute.

My purpose here is modest. It is to identify and explore some of the issues which arise in the relationship between democracy and IT. If democracy is defined as a political system in which citizens govern themselves, then the question is whether, and in what way, IT affects both the opportunity for popular control and the nature of the choices that the electorate faces.

The most commonly cited issues in the discussion of IT concern:

1. The distribution of *power* and *resources* within and between countries, following the introduction and development of IT — the power of IBM versus the power of national governments, 'sovereignty at bay' as Vernon (1973) described it;
2. The impact of IT on the organisation and form of *interests* in society — the creation, for example, of a disenfranchised sector of the permanently unemployed;
3. The consequences of IT on the availability of, and access to, *information* — the promise of electronic democracy versus the threat of electronic tyranny;
4. The *ideological* and *cultural* impact of IT on the self-image of individuals and on the ethos of society.

All these issues bear directly on arguments about, and theories of, democracy. Their relevance will, of course, vary according to the model of democracy subscribed to: an advocate of direct/participatory democracy will not view IT in the same way as a supporter of indirect/representative democracy. It is also the case that IT's impact on democracy will depend on how IT is understood and explained. In the space available it is impossible to do justice to such issues. Instead, my intention is to discuss IT under the four headings suggested above — power and resources; interests; information; and ideology and culture — and then in the concluding section to make some tentative remarks about the implications of IT for democracy, and to beg the general question of whether there is any need to redesign the technology, or redefine the democracy, or both.

POWER AND RESOURCES

The relationship between power, resources and technology is becoming increasingly apparent, if by no means simple. 'Technology', writes Jill Hills, 'is a power resource. Technological leads in crucial industrial processes provide the fuel for national economic power, which, in turn, leads to international political power' (Hills, 1983, p. 203). IT in both its use and development has raised again the issues of national sovereignty and the autonomy of States in relation to multinational corporations.

One of the characteristics of all forms of democracy is the assumption that the duly elected government has the power to give effect to its popular mandate. Many writers have, of course, suggested that the sovereignty of governments is often constrained by a variety of practical, political and economic factors. Such commentators, however, have usually felt able to offer reforms which would enable sovereignty to be re-established — by, for example, withdrawal from the European Community (EC) or by tariff barriers. What IT has done, it might be argued, is to add greatly to the constraints upon government autonomy whilst at the same time making reform either ineffective or irrelevant.

Typically, communications networks are State-controlled or monopoly-controlled, but this apparent centralisation of power disguises a reality in which control is dispersed. Controlling the production and implementation of IT is not simply a matter of managing a market and natural resources. That may have been true of the arguments for public ownership in the 1930s, but IT cannot be so easily accommodated. The public/democratic control of, say, coal raises quite different problems from those raised by IT. Where coal is a national resource which can be exploited with established technologies and distributed through existing markets and mechanisms, IT is developed in an international market by those with expertise and resources over which national governments can have only limited control.

The OCED report (1983) on *Telecommunications* argued that national sovereignty in relation to such technologies is impossible. The nature of the international competition, together with the costs and complexities involved, lead inevitably to the need for increasing liberalisation of trade. Countries, therefore, are advised to abandon hope of developing a national telecommunications industry, and to concentrate instead only on those technologies in which 'they have their greatest competitive advantage' (OECD, 1983, p. 82). These pressures for the liberalisation of international trade, with their consequences for national sovereignty, are increased by trends in the international market. Hills (1984) has drawn attention to the way in which the liberalisation of the American IT market has tended to increase Europe's vulnerability to penetration by companies such as AT & T (Bell) and IBM.

Paradoxically, as governments have lost power to the multinational market leaders in IT, they have come under increasing pressure to advance the cause of IT in their own countries. The dilemma is nicely captured by the report written for the French government by Nora and Minc (1981). Explaining the predicament facing the government, they write:

> weakness in technological know-how and the absence of manufacturers ready to take the risks in such a venture make state action difficult . . . Even if action in this direction were decided on, a double contradiction remains between the need for state support and the need for a dynamic sector. [Nora and Minc, 1981, p. 110]

British government policy for the development of IT has embodied the tensions identified by Nora and Minc. Since the mid-1970s both Labour and Conservative governments have encouraged the production and implementation of IT on the grounds that it is vital to the UK's fortunes. When Kenneth Baker was Minister of Information Technology he had little doubt of the importance of IT: 'the message is automate or liquidate' (Baker, 1982, p. 10). Furthermore, as Mrs Thatcher acknowledged, the propagation of IT depended on 'the central role that Government must play in promoting its development and application' (quoted in Howkins, 1982, p. 34). A similar logic led the 1974–9 Labour government, through the National Enterprise Board (NEB), to set up Inmos. Inmos was a company whose task was to develop and make microchips to rival those being made in the USA and Japan (Benson and Lloyd, 1983). Three-quarters of Inmos's funding came from the NEB, the rest from private investors. In a sense this 25 percent was the price paid for the government's lack of expertise and experience in microelectronics; the government needed the private sector. And it was the existence of this private involvement, together with the fact that Inmos competed as a commercial enterprise in the open market, that disposed the Thatcher government, with its political opposition to the public sector, to sell Inmos to the private sector, where it was bought by Thorn–EMI.

However, the sale of Inmos did not mean the end of State involvement in IT. The Conservative government continued to recognise the need to combine the conflicting practices of State involvement and private competition. The Tory equivalent to Inmos has been the Alvey programme. Under this the government is committed to providing half the research costs for private companies (Plessey, GEC, ICI and RACAL) to work on projects with good commercial prospects or useful administrative applications.

Alvey and Inmos are examples of attempts to manage a complex and competing set of political and practical considerations. Despite their different ideological commitments, both governments recognised the limits of their own ability to create and administer the new technology. However they also acknowledged that without State intervention that technology was unlikely to be introduced, with, in their view, dire consequences for the country's economy and, by implication, their electoral future. In other words, British government policy on IT has involved a commitment of public funds with only limited control over its use. This dependent relationship applies both nationally and internationally, and has an obvious impact on our understanding of what democracy means and how it can be operated.

Although governments may rationalise their policies differently, and although those policies may diverge in important respects, there is an implicit underlying agreement: that it is better to develop IT, whatever the concessions involved, than to be without it. Sir Ieuan Maddock, former Chief Scientist at the Department of Industry, voiced the common conviction that unless the UK developed its own IT industry, the country would become 'a technological colony of large offshore companies who will determine what products are made, where, and when, and how high or low the national standard of living should be' (Large, 1984). In adopting this argument, several other arguments are rejected. These include the case for a no-growth, green economy, and the case for an entirely free market. At the same time it accepts the limited effectiveness of government in the international economy. Partly it is the terms of that economy, and the policies of States and corporations in the international market, that determine the government's choices. This creates one dependence relationship. But another is established by the governments' reliance on the technical expertise and resources in the private sector.

The conditions under which the technology is developed raise real problems for democracy — problems about accountability in the use of public monies, about control over the development of the technology, about sovereign power in an international economy. These questions may not be simply matters of political organisation; they may also be intrinsic to the technology itself.

Furthermore, the impact of IT is not felt just in the development stage; it also applies to its use. We must consider the argument of those who claim that telecommunications are being (re)organised to the advantage of particular commercial interests. Take, for example, the introduction of cellular radio. The available frequencies were allocated to two consortia for a period of twenty-five years. The significance of this decision, as Golding and Murdock (1983, p. 33) point out, is that it 'prevents them [the scarce frequencies] being used to develop public services such as neighbourhood radio'. A more recent decision to put a hold on the promised development of community radio, together with the increase in charges for private telephones, adds to the impression that national communications networks are being used to serve commercial or monopoly interests. Cable TV, while intended to increase choice and access, 'will mainly operate as an extra distribution channel for the commodities produced by the major media corporations' (Golding and Murdock, 1983, p. 35). A similar skewing of telecommunications policy has been observed at the international level.

The application of IT also has implications for the relations between nations, in particular between less-developed and developed countries. The divide between these nations, and the problems it raises for democracy — where are the boundaries of a political community? — are best illustrated by the example of satellites in space. Accepting for the moment the crucial importance of information for the development of nations, and given the role played by space-based technology in this, then the distribution of satellite resources takes on considerable importance. The present use of space is dominated by the developed nations, who both occupy the limited resource provided by space and control the technology itself (Murphy, 1983; Marsh, 1985).

Michael Laver (1984) has drawn attention to the special political implications of the scarcity and cost of geostationary satellite technology. First, the development and use of the technology have been dominated by private interests, confined to the developed world. Second, a fair distribution of the resources available requires and depends on 'some form of international collective action, indeed by collective ownership' (Laver, 1984, p. 66). The problems of producing such a solution are, however, considerable (Laver, 1986).

Just as the development of IT subjects governments to a double bind (they cannot function with IT or without it), so satellites raise a similar dilemma. On the one hand, satellites make possible a new cultural and political pluralism, and allow for the breakdown of national barriers; on the other, they make it possible for existing global divisions to be reinforced, and for the erosion of national sovereignty. More important, the problems of control they pose are similar — if even more complex — to those which apply at the national level. Once again the reach of national government fails to match the task of public control. This problem was anticipated by Karl Kaiser, who wrote in the early 1970s: 'Science policy, particularly in the new fields of electronics . . . and outer space, is an area in which European governments indulge in animated competition that is barely controlled by their parliaments' (Kaiser, 1970–71, p. 361). Or, as Stanley Hoffman has argued, in drawing out the theoretical implications of international dependence, 'while distributive justice is no longer purely an internal concern, our external reach is limited' (Hoffman, 1981, p. 185).

But even if national governments were to be in a position to control IT development and use, there still remains the question of what priorities should apply in exercising this power. In order to judge the democratic use of power in the management of IT and to ensure that all preferences have access to the decision-making process, political theorists require to know how interests are distributed in society. And it is precisely in this endeavour that the political scientists once again confront the impact of IT.

INTERESTS

One of the commonest arguments about the consequences of IT for democracy has focused on the distribution of interests in society. IT has been held responsible for disrupting the mechanisms by which wealth is distributed in a liberal democratic society, and that it has led to the centralisation of political power and the disenfranchising of sections of society (CSE Microelectronics Group, 1980; Jordan, 1981; Albury and Schwartz, 1982; Kaplinsky, 1984). In other words, it is contended that IT threatens to undermine the processes by which popular will and popular power are expressed in a liberal democratic State. There are other writers, with whom I shall not deal here but whose arguments should be borne in mind, who welcome the increase in structural unemployment as heralding the leisure society, or who see the deskilling of workers as a necessary and desirable step towards undermining the illegitimate power of organisations such as trades unions. As the often quoted, much maligned and now late Lord Spens once said, 'Silicon chips do not belong to unions. They do not go on strike. They do not ask for more and more pay' (House of Lords Debates, 20 June 1979, vol. 400, col. 968).

Albury and Schwartz are typical of that group of writers who focus on the use of microelectronics to deskill workers and to weaken their industrial power. They argue, for example, that the Minos system used to automate coal-mining has less to do with safety and efficiency than with class and control: 'The Minos system, by transferring control of machines from the face to a central office, will simultaneously deskill the surface workers and permit management to pace and control work as they see fit' (Albury and Schwartz, 1982, p. 153).

Brian Murphy (1983) uses a similar argument in his discussion of modern communications technology. Although cable television has been introduced into the UK as an additional form of entertainment, its real purpose, suggests Murphy, is to serve business interests (pp. 128–9). Or, as the government sponsored Information Technology Advisory Panel (ITAP) reported, 'we are convinced that there are powerful economic and industrial arguments for encouraging cable systems in the UK' (quoted in Hawkins, 1982, p. 64). From this perspective, IT is seen as a device for advancing particular interests in society at the expense of others. The point is not to focus on the *commercial* interests served by the introduction of such technology, but rather to dwell on its impact on the organisation and access of *political* interests. The problem of unemployment is seen, in part, to be one of disenfranchisement.

This aspect of IT is well exemplified in the literature on the impact of IT on women. The effects of IT on women are not identical to those on men. As one report concluded:

> There is a systematic relationship between the adoption of microelectronics, job losses for women who work in organisational hierarchies and the creation of new, technical jobs which are generally taken up by men. [SPRU Women and Technology Studies, 1985, p. 217]

In returning women to the home IT denies them the opportunity to organise collectively or to share in the public realm. This private existence increases the liklihood of State/male manipulation and control (Huws, 1985, pp. 18–22). The reorganisation of the form and practice of employment can be seen to alter the opportunity and ability of people to exercise control over the distribution of wealth (and power) in society, whatever the formal constitution suggests (Plant, 1984, pp. 16–17).

Bill Jordan (1981) argues that the extensive use of IT leads to a general restructuring of society. Recalling Huxley's vision of the future, Jordan anticipates a world in which there are three classes of people: (1) the technical, scientific and political elite of designers and planners; (2) the machine minders, charged with ministering to the needs of the technology; and (3) the unemployed, the old, and the sick. This last group, because they make no direct contribution to the production process, and because their predicament is a structural fact rather than a temporary aberration, find it increasingly difficult to lay claim to resources in society. Not only are they unable to use their labour power to extract their rewards, their claims come increasingly to involve 'charity'. Unemployment benefit, for example, cannot be justified either as an incentive to work or as a way of managing adjustments in the labour market. Without a consensually accepted notion of justice, the legitimacy of the group's claims will be eroded, while, at the same time, the elite, who can claim to be the creators of the national cake, make increasingly large demands on it for themselves. In one of the starkest expositions of this argument, Hazel Henderson wrote:

> The microprocessor has finally repealed the labour theory of values; there is really no possibility now of maintaining the fiction that human beings can be paid in terms of their labour. The link between jobs and income has been broken. [Quoted in Jones, 1982, p. 1]

Even writers who are given to less dramatic predictions emphasise the need for radical change in political thought and practice in order to accommodate the impact of IT on the industrial and social structure of society (see, for example, Gill, 1985, chapter 7).

What is suggested by these arguments is that the problems for democracy generated by IT are not just those of unemployment. IT has a further effect upon the kinds of interests in society and the way they are organised. In so far as IT leads to a restructuring of the job market and an increase in unemployment, it highlights and exacerbates those problems of legitimacy which liberal democratic societies constantly face (Connolly, 1985). Whether IT is the *cause* of such problems is less clear. In drawing attention to IT's effects on the distribution and power of interests in society, analysts may simply be identifying the way in which IT acts as an instrument of ends already endemic to the system. As one group of researchers wrote, following their account of women's experience of IT, 'It is difficult to imagine how microelectronics technology can, in itself, be sexist. On the other hand, we know that the organisation of our society is exactly that' (SPRU Women and Technology Studies, 1985, p. 217). Other writers are less sanguine about the technology, arguing that it poses particular problems for democracy which cannot be reduced to underlying trends or forces (Winner, 1985). Whatever is the case, resolving this argument, and addressing the problems entailed by changes in the distribution and character of interests in society, must be of immediate importance to the development of a coherent theory of democracy for the modern world. But, once again, the difficulties do not end here. Democracy is not just about the distribution of interests in society, it is also about the information available to those interests.

INFORMATION

Arguments about democracy and IT cannot end with reflections about the organisation of interests in society. It must also take account of the medium through which those interests are formed and articulated. Shirley Williams (1985, p. 204) one of the few mainstream politicians to take the impact of IT seriously, has written, 'The constraints on information are no longer technological. They are political and commercial, and deliberately imposed because those in powerful positions want to keep information in their own hands.' Or, as Richard Neustadt (1985, p. 567) suggests, the spread of IT has speeded up the fragmentation of American political parties and the rise to power of interest groups who are able to use IT to target and manage particular constituencies.

To state the obvious, IT affects the form and availability of information in society. From one point of view, IT adds to the store of information available to ordinary citizens, and thereby improves the quality of democracy. From another perspective, IT increases the store of information available to central government, and thereby enhances its ability to control its subjects.

David Burnham's *The Rise of the Computer State* (1983) is a comprehensive statement of the view that the new technology advances the cause of State tyranny. He seems to have little doubt that it is technology which is responsible for undermining democracy. Simply, his argument is that 'telecommunications equipment and computers have tended to centralise the power held by the top officials in both government and private industry'(p. 13). Burnham is not alone in his view that modern forms of information collection and storage are inimical to certain democratic rights (see also Weeramantry, 1983). His argument is based on two sets of assumptions. The first concerns the nature of the technology: the problems of checking and controlling the use of information stored in computers. The second concerns the character of the political system: the tendency for those in power to advance their control by whatever means are available to them.

As more and more information — about citizen purchases, transactions, services and movements — is acquired and stored in data banks, so the temptation to use this material for State ends becomes irresistible. Once things become possible, the argument runs, they tend to become 'necessary' (Burnham, p. 33). Burnham quotes Abraham Maslow's saying that 'When the only tool you have is a hammer, everything begins to look like a nail' (p. 151).

In Burnham's view, the spread of computers has enabled the National Security Agency to dominate our society should it ever decide such action is necessary' (p. 144). This same trend has also made it possible for politicians to manipulate voters by way of targeting techniques and the selective use of information. Burnham is suspicious too of 'interactive' telecommunications. Although they appear to allow for direct participation by individual citizens, the technology always tends to favour the more powerful actor: the State or the politician. Burnham's worries about privacy and accountability in the use of computerised information, about the motives and interests of those in power, and about the nature of technology itself, are such as to incline him to see IT as a threat to democracy.

Campbell and Connor (1986) express similar worries, but without Burnham's implicit determinism. For them, the threat of data banks stems only indirectly from the technology; the real source of worry is 'the attitude of administrators' (p. 51) or 'the nature of means-testing' (p. 106). Such factors, when tied to the power of computers, do undermine political rights and civil liberties.

Quite different conclusions are drawn by other writers who have also observed the effect of IT on information. Garratt and Wright (1980) have suggested that the new communications technology 'should allow decision-making to be faster, more responsive to events, and theoretically enable *all* members of a unit to be consulted rather than just one delegate'. They anticipate a day when politics will be 'the occupation of the many rather than the personal gamesmanship of the few' (p. 493). Where Garratt and Wright recognise that at present IT is not put to the use they envisage, Stonier (1983) argues that the technology, almost automatically, leads to the extension of democracy and to the diminution of State power. The spread of the telephone in the USSR, for example, has provided the opportunity for dissidents to communicate and organise more effectively. Where meetings and publications are easily controlled, telephone communications pose much greater problems. In the West, too, it is possible to see the development of cheap radio, cassette and computer equipment as enabling individuals to rival the power of State and commercial monopolies. This may appear in the formally recognised form of public access channels on cable TV in the USA (see Kellner, 1985), or citizen band radio (see the film *Citizen Band*), or in the informal practices established by pirate radio stations, computer hackers, and bootleg cassette recordings (see Hall, 1984 and 1985).

In his defence of 'strong democracy' Barber specifically ties his political proposals to the technological possibilities of IT: 'The capabilities of the new technology can be used to strengthen civic education, guarantee equal access to information, and tie individuals and institutions into networks that will make real participatory discussion and debate possible across great distances' (Barber, 1984, p. 274). But in advocating this use of IT, Barber recognises that certain conditions have to apply for the technology to be used effectively.

While IT enhances the potential for greater freedom of expression, and more extensive circulation and exchange of information, there is a need to recognise the *conditions* which allow the technology to operate in this way. Although the technology does, indeed, shape the possibilities in any given situation and the technology is itself a consequence of other factors. The freedon of information and expression which IT promises depends on the creation of a context, and of safeguards which prevent abuse. In the same way that the fair use of space and satellite technology depends on control exercised by a suitable international agency, so democratic mass communication depends on the creation of bodies which can monitor and discipline the use of broadcast media (see Tannsjo, 1985).

In assessing the potential gains or dangers of IT, it is clearly necessary to avoid both technical determinism (as represented by either Burnham or Stonier), and social determinism (as represented by Campbell and Connor). Computer technology provides for qualitatively different ways of storing and handling information, ways that were previously impossible for example, full text retrieval (FTR), the ability to alter the coding of information after it has been stored, appears to pose almost insurmountable problems for those who seek democratic control of the use of information, simply because no rules can by established for the use and collection of data (Lindop, 1978). However, the very existence of FTR, and the problems it poses are a function not just of the technology but of the context in which it operates. As Bolter points out, there is no neat correlation between technology and political ideology:

> The premise of Orwell's *1984* [sic] was the marriage of totalitarian purpose with modern technology. But the most modern technology, computer technology, may well be incompatible with the totalitarian monster . . . It is no accident that the autocratic regimes of Eastern Europe today are almost untouched by the computer age. [Bolter 1984, p 225]

Bolter goes on to argue (*contra* Stonier) that although computers 'make hierarchical communication and control far easier', they also (*contra* Burnham) 'work against the fundamental sense of purpose, the absolute dedication of the party line, which is the core of the autocratic state'. He concludes, 'If anything, the great political danger of the computer age is a new definition of anarchy' (1984, p. 225). Such a view is confirmed by the practical experience of David Howell, who, reflecting on his time as a Minister, writes, 'information technology is turning out to be the agent not of a new uniformity but of variety and disorder. Things are becoming less controllable, less programmable, less easy to boss about from the bureaucratic centre' (Howell, 1985, p. 85).

The development of IT, according to Bolter, reflects and embodies changes in culture and ideology which cannot be neatly fitted into existing political structures and practices. Computer technology is altering the citizen and society in such a way as to require a rethinking of the assumptions which underpin much political thought, including democratic theory.

IDEOLOGY AND CULTURE

What the writers and ideas considered under this (not altogether satisfactory) heading have in common is the suggested that IT is transforming the way in which individuals in Western society think and act. The conclusions drawn from this broad observation differ, but there is an agreement that some of the traditional assumptions about the democratic process are being undermined or revised, for good or ill.

In his novel *The Tin Men* (1966) Michael Frayn satirises the views of those who celebrate the advent of the computer. One character reflects on the possibilities that computers open up:

> Then you'll start producing a programme for automating the football results. Again, it had to come. Professional football is becoming increasingly uneconomical, but the pools industry has to carry on . . .

Paying twenty-two men to do nothing but make a random choice between win, lose and draw is economic madness. [Frayn, 1966, p. 42]

This process, by which computers are deemed to replace essentially 'human' abilities or qualities, is a common theme of those who consider the ideological impact of IT. In his book *The Slumbering Sentinels* Weeramantry (1983) writes:

> Technology not only dominates politics, it also shapes nearly all attitudes and patterns of conduct. Technology sets the life of modern people in an atmosphere of waste which promotes further waste, which in turn feeds the technological and commercial machine. Political life and political decision making become geared to this wasteful way of life. It is one of the possible causes of world conflict and hence the end of civilisation. [p. 207]

In a similar vein Joseph Weizenbaum (1984) concentrates on the way in which computers advance the cause of instrumental reasoning. For him the predominant fear is that society will come to be organised by computers and their 'logic'. Decisions will be taken in the name of a narrowly defined efficiency. He writes of 'the mechanisation of reason and of language' (p. 252), arguing that reliance upon computers in government allows responsibilty to be devolved to the machine. Not only are computers being used to take decisions, they also embody the paradigm of 'rational' decision-making. They are impartial, reliable and efficient. Computers are increasingly being used to replace humans; or they are used by humans to excuse their own failings or ambitions. For dystopians like Weizenbaum and Weeramantry computer technology is leading to the imposition of a computer culture in which democracy cannot hope to survive. For them the arguments about artificial intelligence (AI) have (or are being) settled in favour of those who see human intelligence as an inefficient form of computer technology. The computer has become the model of human excellence. In these circumstances, it is almost inevitable that power and responsibility will shift from us to the computer.

While these dystopian writers draw doom-filled conclusions from their observations, other commentators look on hopefully. For every pessimist decrying artificial intelligence there is a utopian for whom it is the logical consequence of human progress (Jastrow, 1978). Although such writers see little point in denying or directing progress, they are prepared to argue, against the dystopians, that computer technology advances the cause of democracy. IT furnishes the conditions either for efficient, rational decisions or for mass participation.

Both sides of this debate, I suspect, are familiar, and their failings need not detain us here. Both share a similar tendency towards technological determinism, expressed in their exaggerated respect for the power and perfection of the technology. Too little attention is paid either to the details of the technology or to the context in which it operates. Were more concern given to such things, the dramatic generalisations which each side employs would look much less convincing. Take the dystopians. There is a tension between the ideal, self-sufficient world against which the present is unfavourably compared and the inevitablity with which they invest their account of technical change. How are powerless people to change an all-powerful technology? A similar contradiction is noted by Marshall Berman (1984, p. 83): 'The paradoxical reality which escapes most of these writers is that in modern society only the most extravagant and systematic "thinking big" can open up channels for "thinking small".' Berman's wider purpose is to argue for the need to understand modern life better, and to appreciate more clearly its limits and possibilities. For him the development of technology is largely a consequence of choices made by modern men and women: 'If scientific and technological cadres have accumulated vast powers in modern society, it is only because their visions and values have echoed, amplified and realised our own' (p. 85). Development leads inevitably to regret for what is lost and cannot be recreated; those who resent the intrusions of technology recognise only one side of the choice that has been made.

Berman's argument should not be seen as an unreflective advocacy of technological change. Instead, it focuses attention upon the fact that the modern world is partly constituted by conscious choices with undesirable but unavoidable costs. It follows from this that democratic theorists, rather than building their models from materials selected from a world that no longer exists (if it ever did) should draw on those materials which now lie to hand. However, adopting this approach does not lead inevitably to the technocratic vision of the optimists. What it does lead to is a need to recognise the opportunities and constraints which IT introduces into the world we inhabit.

It is this spirit which informs Bolter's *Turing's Man* (1984). (The title refers to Alan Turing, the mathematician who first conceived the theoretical possibility of the computer and of artificial intelligence. Bolter acknowledges that IT will change modern culture, but he is not a determinist. 'The computer he writes, 'is giving us a new definition of man, as an "information processor", and of nature, as "information to be processed"' (p. 13). The computer, like the clock before it, constitutes a 'defining technology'; that is, it 'develops links, metaphorical or otherwise, with a culture's science, philosophy, or literature' (p. 11). But the computer does not act deterministically; it does not embody a single ideology or set of assumptions; it cannot sustain a single world vision, whether it involves 'instrumental reason' or 'progress'. Or, more accurately, those terms do not have the meaning attributed to them by the dystopian–utopian debate.

'Progress' within computer culture, for example, does not entail ceaseless use of resources in an endless pursuit of material growth. Such a notion of progress belongs to a world in which the concept of infinity exists. As Newton was replaced by Einstein, so infinity (space) was replaced by the finite (the speed of light). The computer is the embodiment of this shift in perceptions. The computer program is a set of repetitive tasks in pursuit of an indentifiable goal. Computers can work only towards a definitive goal and within a finite time — 'nothing good is endless in the computer world' (Bolter, 1984, p. 121). In so far as the computer is a defining technology, then its characteristics inform the surrounding culture. This encourages a new, less arrogant notion of progress:

> In the end, the idea of progress through repetition favours stability over growth . . . Computer specialists, along with other engineers, are sympathetic to efforts at conservation and control, in society at large as well as in their own work. Their experience of programming, shared by millions of educated people, is helping to change our culture's view of progress . . . [p. 123]

Other features of the computer's mode of operation further enhance this progress.

Where dystopians and utopians anticipate the replacement of the book by the computer, Bolter draws our attention to a more fundamental change. The book, he argues, made memory redundant; everything could be looked up. With computer-stored information, memory is revived in a form that resembles its pre-literary form, when memory was the way in which knowledge was stored. Memory is the key to knowledge, and knowledge is essential to control over the world (p. 162). Where Weizenbaum (1984, p. 238) writes of computer technology as eliminating history, Bolter sees it as reviving history, and in doing so, as reinforcing the will to conserve (pp. 185–6).

But the sympathy for conservation that is engendered is not typical of either traditional conservatism or contemporary conservationists. The computer gives effect to a radical liberalism in which no ultimate purpose can be assumed. In the world of the computer there can be no infinite progress, but neither is there any prescribed end. Computer technology and programming pander to the idea of 'the world as a game in the mind of a playful god' (Bolter, p. 188). The computer's ability to simulate any number of possible worlds, to act in any number of ways, reinforces the idea that nothing is fixed or fundamental about who we are or how we live. This is precisely the point Berman makes in his account of the experience of modernism, and which Bolter makes in stressing that many of the conservative/conservationist visions of the past are based on a highly selective reading of history (Bolter, 1984, p. 216). 'Turing's man' is the result of this process. 'Turing's man treats ideas in plastic terms: he shapes and re-shapes them ... Turing's man ... does not speak of "destiny" but rather of "options"' (pp. 222–5).

If Bolter is right about the computer and its role as a defining technology, then the culture which it is being ushered in may be more, not less, compatible with the principles of liberal democracy. The spirit of pluralism and scepticism embodied by the computer exactly suits the assumptions enshrined in liberal democracy. At the same time the new computer culture favours the urge to conserve, which not only fits well with a general concern over finite resources, but also helps resolve the problem of fair distribution, which, typically, liberal democracy cannot manage without growth (Plant, 1984). While Frayn's vision of a mechanised football season is unlikely to attract much sympathy (except among cricket lovers), the same line of thought does open up genuine possibilities of diminishing the demand on certain scarce goods or easing the pressure on other services. On-line medical consultancy, for example, can reorganise the good of medical attention in such a way as to create a new set of conditions governing its use and value.

It is also true that the problems of maintaining a liberal democracy under conditions of low or no growth cannot be solved simply by an appeal either to computers or to the associated culture. The problems of social division and democratic control of the implementation of new technology remain problems which cannot be resolved without major changes in economic and political institutions and practice, and in conditions where powerful interests seek to prevent such change.

CONCLUSION

There are perhaps no real conclusions to be drawn from this necessarily sketchy survey of the issues that are coming to concern political scientists. Indeed, it would be presumptuous to make any such attempt. On the other hand, it would be cowardly not to end with a few tentative remarks about the implications of IT for thinking about democracy.

The most obvious point should be made first. Much depends on how democracy itself is conceived. The significance of IT for representative democracy is not the same as for participatory democracy, and it is intriguing to observe that advocates of the latter tend to be most critical of the present uses of IT, but most optimistic about its potential.

A superficial glance at the literature on democracy and IT might suggest that the only aspect of IT that is of any significance concerns its ability to disseminate or manipulate information. It is the vision of an electronic democracy with instant polling and on-line accountability, or of electronic totalitarianism with permanent surveillance, that most frequently accompanies analysis of IT's political impact. There is, of course, nothing necessarily surprising or wrong in this observation, but there is a danger in being caught up in this one feature of IT. Firstly, it rests on a rather simple, and potentially dangerous, account of democracy as instant populism (see Neustadt, 1985). Secondly, it takes as given the form and organisation of the technology; it asks few questions about how computer design and ownership limit the political choices available.

Any discussion of IT and democracy must, therefore, pay due attention to the system by which information is generated, transmitted and owned. In tackling these questions it is necessary to consider the principles which (should) govern relations between States and which determine the extent of political boundaries. Kaiser (1970–71) observed fifteen years ago that 'the intermeshing of decision making across national frontiers and the growing multinationalisation of formerly domestic issues are inherently incompatible with the traditional framework of domestic control' (p. 356). Furthermore, he speculated that the consequence of this incommensurability, if left unmodified, would be 'technocratic rule' (p. 367). Certainly, as we have seen, the present character of the IT economy places governments under the apparently conflicting and irresolvable pressures of a double bind. One step in the resolution of these difficulties seems to require, in Charles Beitz's words, a 'shift from statist to global conceptions of world order' (1979, p. 176), a point echoed by Laver (1986).

Just as the information side of IT cannot be separated from the political economy of the technology, so it is with IT and the interests which organise around it. It is clearly important for theorists of democracy to recognise that while IT may, in one form, democratise information, it may, in another, shift the balance of power between groups in society. The problem for democracy then becomes one of producing mechanisms which represent equally the various interests at play. IT throws into sharp focus a problem that is familiar to students of democracy: how to ensure equality without restricting liberty when the claims of one group are always likely to prevail (even where justice suggests otherwise) due to their strategic or other importance. The forms of employment and unemployment generated via IT pose real problems for the creation of a model of equality that is not mediated through the work ethic.

Finally, however vague or uncertain the cultural or ideological impact of IT, it does suggest an avenue of inquiry which may, among other things, help to resolve some of the problems referred to above. There is undoubtedly something attractive about a modern technology which depends upon an ideology of conservation.

BIBLIOGRAPHY

Albury, D., and Schwartz, J. (1982), *Partial Progress*, Pluto, London.
Baker, K. (1982), *IT and its Impact on Industry and Employment*, Department of Industry, London.
Beitz, C. (1979), *Political Theory and International Relations*, Princeton University Press, Princeton, N.J.
Benson, I., and Lloyd, J. (1983), *New Technology and Industrial Change* Routledge & Kegan Paul, London.
Berman, M. (1984), *All that is solid melts into air*, Verso, London.
Bolter, J. D. (1984), *Turing's Man*, Duckworth, London.
Burnham, D. (1983), *The Rise of the Computer State*, Weidenfeld & Nicolson, London.
Campbell, D., and Connor, S. (1986), *On the Record*, Michael Joseph, London.
Connolly, W. E. (ed.) (1985), *Legitimacy and the State*, Blackwell, Oxford.
CSE Microelectronics Group (1980), *Microelectronics*, CSE Books, London.
Fryan, M. (1966), *The Tin Man*, Fontana, London.
Garratt, J., and Wright, G. (1980), 'Micro is beautiful', in T. Forester, *The Microelectronics Revolution*, Blackwell, Oxford, pp. 448–96.
Gill, C. (1985), *Work, Unemployment and the New Technology*, Polity, Oxford.
Glover, J. (1984), *What Sort of People Should There Be*, Penguin, London.
Golding, P., and Murdock, G. (1983), 'Privatising pleasure', *Marxism Today*, 27 (10), pp. 32–6.
Hall, S. (1984), 'The State: socialism's old caretaker', *Marxism Today*, 28 (11), pp. 24–9.
Hall, S. (1985), 'Realignment for what?', *Marxism Today*, 29 (12), pp. 12–17.
Hardin, R. (ed.) (1985), *Symposium on Ethics and Nuclear Deterrence*, University of Chicago, Chicago, Ill.
Hills, J. (1983), 'Foreign policy and technology', *Political Studies,XXXI*, pp. 205–23.

Hills, J. (1984), 'Dependence and Electronics: Is there an Alternative for Europe?', paper to Political Studies Association Conference, University of Southampton.
Hoffmann, S. (1981), *Democracy beyond Borders*, Syracuse University Press, New York.
Howell, D. (1985), 'IT and relations between government and the public', *Catalyst*, *1* (4), pp. 75–85.
Hawkins, J. (1982), *New Technologies, New Policies?* BFI, London.
Huws, U. (1985), 'Terminal isolation', *Radical Science*, *16*, pp. 9–26.
Jastrow, R. (1978), 'Toward an intelligence beyond man's', *Time*, 20 February, p. 53.
Jones, Barry (1982), *Sleepers, Wake! Technology and the Future of Work*, Wheatsheaf, Brighton.
Jordan, B. (1981), *Automated Poverty*, Routledge & Kegan Paul, London.
Kaiser, K. (1970–71) 'Transnational relations as a threat to the democratic process', in R. Keohane and J. Nye, *Transnational Relations and World Politics*, Harvard University Press, Cambridge, Mass., pp. 356–70.
Kaplinsky, R. (1984), *Automation: the Technology and Society*, Longman, London.
Kellner, D. (1985), 'Public access television', *Radical Science*, *16*, pp. 70–92.
Kenny, A. (1985), *The Logic of Deterrence*, Firethorne, London.
Large, P. (1984), 'Sence is putting cash where your chips are', *Guardian*, 17 April.
Laver, M. (1984), 'The politics of inner space', *European Journal of Political Research*, *12* (1), pp. 59–71.
Laver, M. (1986), 'Public, private and common in outer space', *Political Studies*, *XXXIV* (3), pp. 359–73.
Lindop, N. (1978), *Report of the Committee on Data Protection*, HMSO, Cmnd 7341.
Marsh, P. (1985), *The Space Business*, Penguin, London.
Murphy, B. (1983), *The World Wired Up*, Comedia, London.
Neustadt, R. (1985), 'Electronic politics', in T. Forester, *The Information Technology Revolution*, Blackwell, Oxford, pp. 561–8.
Nora, S., and Minc, A. (1981), *The Computerisation of Society*, MIT Press, Cambridge, Mass.
OECD (1983), *Telecommunications*, OECD, Paris.
Plant, R. (1984), *Equality, Markets and the State*, Fabian Society Pamphlet, London, No. 494.
SPRU Women and Technology Studies (1985), 'Microelectronics and the jobs women do', in W. Faulkner and E. Arnold, *Smothered by Invention*, Pluto, London, pp. 200–1.
Stonier, T. (1983), 'The microelectronic revolution, Soviet political structure, and the future of East West relations', *Politieal Quarterly*, *54*, pp. 137–51.
Tannsjo, T. (1985), 'Against freedom of expression', *Political Studies*, *XXXIII*, pp. 547–59.
Vernon, R. (1973), *Sovereignty at Bay*, Penguin, London.
Weeramantry, C. (1983), *The Slumbering Sentinels*, Penguin, London.
Weizenbaum, J. (1984), *Computer Power and Human Reason*, Penguin, London.
Williams, F. (1982), *The Communications Revolution*, Sage, New York.
Williams, S. (1985), *A Job to Live*, Penguin, London.
Winner, L, (1985), 'Do artifacts have politics?', in D. Mackenzie and J. Wajcman (eds), *The Social Shaping of Technology*, Open University Press, Milton Keynes, pp. 26–38.

The role of the information society conception in IT policy: some international comparisons and a critique

DAVID LYON
Bradford and Ilkley College and the University of Leeds

THE INFORMATION SOCIETY AND PUBLIC POLICY

The information technology (IT) sector is new, and in a state of flux. This is true in all the advanced societies. No one can discern what the key trends will be ten years hence. It is hardly surprising, then, that there should be no really coherent 'public policy' in relation to IT at least in the UK and the USA. Its importance to public policy has been recognised, for instance, in the curious situation whereby the Manpower Services Commission (MSC) has initiated changes in educational curricula. The 'needs of industry' must be rapidly met, it seems. But policies which do exist are often *ad hoc*, contradictory, or with no single clear direction. In the UK, for instance, cable television developments fall between two different government departments, the Home Office and the Department of Trade and Industry.

Within this confusion, however, some kinds of proposals stand out, because they sound as if more than mere pragmatism is at work. I have in mind those claims, often alluded to in policy discourse, which refer to the 'information society'. The idea is that advanced societies are experiencing a transformation to an information society, economically based on the exploitation of microelectronics, computing and telecommunications technologies. But what is the status of the information society concept? Is it a useful social analytical tool, a utopian social forecast, or what?

Without disputing the significance of IT for economic development in advanced societies, I wish to argue that the information society concept at present provides neither a coherent tool for social analysis, nor an adequate set of social goals. At the same time, the social and political challenge presented by the diffusion of IT makes urgent the quest of precisely such appropriate analytical concepts and proper social goals.

In what follows, I begin by noting ways in which the coming of the information society is linked with policy decisions, referring in particular to industrial location, and to technically orientated innovation within education. I say 'linked with' to leave open the question of whether this is a rational predicate of policy or merely an ideological rationalisation which obscures some other interests. I then outline the information society concept, discuss its origins, and suggest where its main weaknesses lie. I argue that there are really two information societies — an analytical and a utopian — which are distinguishable. I conclude by stressing the importance of examining both their relation to each other, and the relevance to policy-making of the issues raised by each.

INFORMATION SOCIETY IN PUBLIC POLICY

Despite various national and cultural variations, the idea that the advanced societies are entering a new phase of history is a common theme of economic and political discourse. The concept of an information society is intended to evoke a new image, contrasting with the old image of industrial society. Just as the industrial era was ushered in by the Industrial Revolution, so we are currently in the throes of an 'information revolution'. There are many hints in policy that the outcome of this revolution will be a information-based or information-centred society. The British Department of Trade and Industry, for instance, uses a booklet entitled *Information Technology: the Age of Electronic Information* to encourage firms in their use of microelectronics-based technologies. IT will, they say, 'revolutionise the handling, storing and processing of information'. It will also 'transform our way of living' (DTI, 1982 p. 1).

This conviction about social transformation permeates other policy background documents as well. The Science Council of Canada produced a report for the Ministry of Supply for Science and Technology, entitled *Planning Now for the Information Society: Tomorrow is Too Late*' (1982). More recently the same body issued *The Uneasy Eighties: the Transition to a information Society* (Cordell, 1985). Microelectronics advances 'are causing a worldwide technological revolution which all societies must accommodate' (Science Council of

Canada 1982, p. 10). In Canada's case, the 'ability to make a successful transition to an efficient, integrated information society depends on the strength of the telecommunications infrastructure' (1982, p. 52).

Many similar such reports (including the Canadian) quote the well-known French study by Simon Nora and Alain Minc: *The Computerisation of Society*. (1980). Interesting enough, this report, whilst stressing the revolutionary nature of the new technologies along with their social and political impacts, also calls for a more cautious and measured approach: 'In order to make the information society possible, it is necessary to have knowledge but also to have time. The reciprocal learning process of disciplines and aspirations takes place slowly...' (Nora and Minc, 1980, p. 141).

It is arguable that Japan was the first to use the term information society in the context of technological change and policy formulation. In the 1970s several commentators wrote about *Johoka* (information society) as the social equivalent to biological evolution. As the brain and nervous system as are the most highly developed aspects of human biology, so the information industry represents the peak of social evolution. Yoneji Masuda wrote 'The Plan for Information Society: a National Goal Toward the Year 2,000' (1971) and many of the ideas it contains have been adopted by the Ministry of International Trade and Industry (MITI) in Japan. He sees his work on the information society as both an analysis of what is happening, and a 'blueprint' for policy information (p. 3).

Of course, references to France and Japan raise important questions about how far information society ideas and ideals have been realised in practise. French development of *l'informatique* scarcely resembles the Nora and Minc recommendations. And views highly sceptical of the Japanese *Johoka* policy implementation have been expressed (for example, by Woronoff, 1985). The mere existence of social and economic goals guarantees nothing.

At its simplest, then, a number of different observers — analysts and policy-makers — insist that the diffusion of information technologies will bring about an information society. The production, processing and distribution of information is becoming a central activity of this society. Thus it is not surprising to hear the claim that 'The concept of the "information society" proposed in the works of such American writers as Machlup (1980), Bell (1973), and Porat (1977) is providing one foundation for a new paradigm for policy research and analysis' (Edgar and Rahim, 1983 p. 5).

Leaving on one side, for the moment, the questions of how exactly the new technologies will produce a new society, the sense in which it can be described as a new society, and the extent to which all will benefit from the diffusion of IT, I offer a couple of illustrations of the practical import of the information society concept.

Industrial location
If the development of IT is the technical prerequisite for an information society, then how best may IT development be fostered? The 1980s have witnessed one important answer to this question in the establishment of technology parks (along with science parks and upgraded industrial parks). This now familiar concept involves the integration on one site (or at least within geographically adjacent areas) of three factors: universities, high technology entrepreneurs and production units.

The model to be emulated is Silicon Valley in Northern California, which is where Stanford University's now legendary Professor Frank Terman first encouraged young engineers to set up their own businesses on the university campus. His policy was one major factor contributing to the huge economic success of microelectronics-based industries in Silicon Valley. The connection between this and theory is put neatly by Larsen and Rogers (1984), 'In an information society the university (particularly the research university... is the central institution, much as the factory was in the previous era of the industrial society' (p. 232).

Following in Silicon Valley's footsteps is a whole bevy of other would-be centres of high-tech based on a university. In the USA, Silicon Prairie, Silicon Mountain, Silicon Beach and others try to replicate Northern California's original efforts, in many cases with State government of city authorities taking the lead in development. The strongest rival to Silicon Valley is, in fact, the area known as Route 128 around Boston. But, of course, the aspiring Silicon Valley clones are not restricted to the USA.

British pundits speak freely of Silicon Glen (Central Scotland), Silicon Fen (Cambridge), and the M4 Corridor as high-tech centres. A recent newspaper report cited the Solent region as the latest 'British Silicon Valley'. Local estate agents are describing Hampshire as 'the California of the UK', and the '20-mile long M27 to the North of Portsmouth and Southampton is becoming its Silicon Valley' (Beresford, 1986). True enough, the area has its research establishments, including the University of Southampton and Portsmouth Polytechnic, firms, like Plessey and Marconi, plus IBM and California's

Hewlett-Packard, and another factor which is also vital to Silicon Valley's history, important defence establishments. It also boasts good communications and (relatively speaking) a pleasant climate.

Elsewhere in Europe can be found similar phenomena. In West Germany, for example, Lothar Speath, the State Prime Minister of Baden–Württemberg, has created three technology parks in the region. They co-operate closely with universities, research foundations and industry in the hope of ensuring that Baden–Württemberg will maintain 'its leading position in the gradual changeover from an industrial to a technological and a computer society' (Tomforde, 1986).

In Japan, where *dirigisme* is more pronounced, a number of 'technopolises' are being established to promote high-tech industries (and to reduce urban overcrowding). Again, these comprise factories, universities, and research institutes as well as workers' housing. MITI is behind these developments and gives authorisation for those prefectures which wish to construct such technopolises. The rise of the technopolis illustrates once more the Japanese desire to be the world's leading information society.

The backdrop to information society enthusiasm is the world recession that has existed since the mid-1970s. (Clearly, this affects countries differently, depending on their economic history. Japan offers obvious contrasts.) Tony Taylor, analysing the British situation, argues that there is a connection between beliefs that we are entering a 'metamorphic phase of human history' (which he associates with Brzenzinski) and the setting up of science and technology parks. The theoretical link is the 'Kondratiev cycle' of technological rejuvenation and its economic spin-offs. Thus, he concludes, ... those parts of the United Kingdom most affected by massive economic decline (inevitably the older industrial cities) are attempting to precipitate Brzenzinski's revolution by clutching at high technology, more particularly science and technology parks, as their sole panacea for future survival' (Taylor, 1983, pp. 72–3).

Whatever the national variations, the point holds that information society hopes are associated with policies for science and technology parks. It is not clear that the optimism associated with such developments is warranted, particularly the promise of employment levels. Nor how these relatively unco-ordinated efforts, and what Taylor calls the 'locational scramble' and 'funding gamble' will contribute to the kind of information society envisaged by Brzenzinski and friends. And lastly, it is doubtful whether those pursuing such policies have examined other — rather less desirable — aspects of social life in the original Silicon Valley before trying to replicate it. I shall return to these questions later.

Educational innovation
The area of education provides a second clear example of the way in which policy may be related to claims that we are entering a new kind of society. A quotation from a publication of the British Microelectronics Programme (MEP) makes the point:

> Our society is on the threshold of a new era — the era of information and automation. The changes which we shall experience as that new era emerges will be profound and will affect every aspect of society. The rate of change is increasing relentlessly and will be unparalleled in the history of mankind. It is the combination of the rate of change and its all-pervasiveness which requires urgent action on the part of everyone concerned with the education of young people. [Dutton, etc. (1984); p. 4].

The very establishment of the MEP (in 1980) was an outcome of government policy relating to information technology. (Its clumsy demise in 1985 illustrates the confusion of long-term policy already alluded.

The economic push towards the redirection of education for the information society is both crucial and controversial. In the UK it was not the Department of Education and Science, but the Department of Trade and Industry which launched the 'Micros in Schools' programme in 1981. This project succeeded in placing a microcomputer in almost every British school by the end of 1984. In 1985 the same department offered a (modest) subsidy for the purchase of school software. Similarly, the Technical and Vocational Education Initiative (TVEI), set up in 1983, is administered by the MSC, again, not a directly educational body. The rationale for this is that a skills shortage exists in relation to the new technologies, and that the education system must make good those skills.

Of course, this economic push factor is not limited to the UK, or to the level of high schools alone. In the USA, the National Commission on Excellence in Education argued that computing should be treated as the 'fourth r'. The number of computers in schools doubled in the year following the publication of this report (Tucker, 1985, p. 12). In other countries the picture is similar. At the higher education level policy is also under pressure from the economy. The notorious Green Paper, *The Development of Higher Education into the 1990s* (1985), emphasised the point that polytechnics, colleges and universities must 'contribute more effectively to the improvement of the performance of the economy' (see also Robins and Webster, 1985).

Once again, the idea that we are at the brink of a new era is used as a kind of inducement to take all possible steps to enter that new society. Within educational institutions, wide divergences of opinion are expressed about many matters, from the relevance of microcomputers to schools (why not minis or mainframe terminals?), to whether technical and vocational education is the best way to develop IT-related skills (see CERI, 1986, pp. 14–15). There is also disagreement (and scepticism) about the extent to which the wider economy should influence the content of education curricula, and fears that the new schemes will be irrelevant to the actual employment structure of the next decades, or that they will accentuate the divisions between C. P. Snow's 'two cultures', or between the 'information rich and information poor'

Both examples — of industrial location and educational innovation — give grounds for thinking that the information society concept requires closer examination, and perhaps clarification and revision.

THE INFORMATION SOCIETY CONCEPT

At the heart of the concept of the information society is the idea that advanced societies are entering a qualitatively different phase of existence. Just as the industrial society differed from the preceeding society, so the information society will be different from the industrial society. The imagery of Alvin Toffler's *Third Wave* (1980) captures nicely this sense of epochal transformation. Of his ten 'megatrends', futurologist John Naisbitt says that 'none is more subtle, yet more explosive, I think, than this first, the megashift from an industrial to an information society' (Naisbitt, 1984 p. 1).

Staying, for a moment, with the analysts who propose a strong version of this thesis, we note that Tom Stonier makes explicit parallels and contrasts between industrial and information societies. His book, *The Wealth of Information* (1983) deliberately echoes the title of Adam Smith's economic manifesto for industrial capitalism (*The Wealth of Nations*, 1976), and he quotes Smith in ways which invite reapplication to the world of IT. In the Japanese context, Masuda asserts that 'The information society will be a new type of human society, completely different from the present industrial society,' (1982, p. 29).

Two major related factors underlie the information society claims. Firstly, that society is becoming increasingly centred on information handling, processing, storage, and dissemination, using microelectronics-based technologies, above all those made available through the convergence of the computer with telecommunications, namely, IT. And secondly, that this shift is reflected in an emerging occupational structure in which the category of 'information workers' has become predominant. The information society appears as an outcome of technological and economic changes.

The British Department of Trade and Industry publication, *Information Technology: the age of Electronic Information* (1982), makes use of just such a line of argument. Another government document is cited, which sees IT as 'a key point in the future growth in the economy'. And it is claimed that ' . . . as many as 65 percent of our working population now earn their living in what may be broadly classified as information occupations' (DTI, 1982, p. 2). The accompanying graph which shows these trends in occupational change is culled, significantly, from the American Bureau of Labor Statistics. We are assured that things are similar in Europe.

At the beginning of the decade a European Community Forecasting and Assessment in the field of Science and Technology (Fast) report predicted that ' . . . in the 1980s the information society could become the most important policy question in organisations and governments alike' (Bjorn-Anderson, 1982, p. xii). Whether or not the report is proved right, the concept of the information society appears to be informing policy debate.

But to what extent is the information society concept unified and coherent? The more visionary and futuristic versions tend to be somewhat optimistic, seeing rising employment prospects or 'computer democracy' as expected benefits of the application of IT. But even the more sober versions that make their way into policy documents frequently lack reference to aspects of the IT an society equation — such as the military impetus to IT development — which are readily demonstrable, and which may not be entirely benign.

The information society concept is fairly coherent (though not beyond critique) in so far as it depends on the seminal work of Daniel Bell and Marc Porat. At the same time, distinctions may be made along the lines of national and cultural variation (the information society idea finds a readier audience in the USA, and considerably more scepticism in countries like West Germany). Added to which, important differences of emphasis may be discerned, as a National Economic Development ment Council (NEDC) report suggests. (Bessant *et al.*, 1985, pp. 12–13) Its authors distinguished between three groups of 'IT futures' forecasters: the first group sees the 'silicon revolution' more as part of a long-term evolutionary process than as heralding a transition to new social formations. They would not use the information society concept at all. The second group is the one to which I have made most reference, that is, those who believe that epochal change is occurring, based precisely upon the 'silicon revolution'. The third group falls between the other two, seeing present changes as 'well-rooted in previous generations of technological innovation', but nevertheless involving nothing less than the 'restructuring of industrial society'. This third group is likely to have sympathies with the revival of interest in Kondratiev's 'long waves' of economic activity. They also may, on occasion, use the information society concept.

Origins of the information society concept
The information society concept has close affinities with the theory of post-industrial society. Daniel Bell, the classical exponent of post-industrialism, also theorised the information society, (Bell, 1980). As Miles and Gershuny (1986) argue, the core of post-industrialism is a 'march through the sectors' in which economic development is a 'progressive shift in the focus of activity' from agriculture to manufacturing to services (p. 18). Within this view, worry about jobs lost through automation was misplaced, because the expanding services sector would soak up displaced labour. At the same time, material needs would be satisfied with less human effort, yielding both more leisure time and increased demand for health and education.

In *The Coming of Post-Industrial Society* (1973) Bell argued that the increased part played by science in the productive process, the rise to prominence of professional, scientific and technical groups, plus the introduction of computer technology are all evidence of a new 'axial principle' at the core of the socio-economic system, namely, the centrality of theoretical knowledge (hence, the importance of the university). The emerging social framework of the information society builds upon this base. Information increasingly becomes a source of added value and thus of wealth. A growing proportion of workers is employed in the 'information' sphere (and here Bell relies on the forecasts of Mark Porat, 1977). As a focus of economic activity, information gradually supplants the service sector.

The key factor enabling analytical discourse to switch from post-industrialism to the information society is the massive growth in the economic significance of IT. What gives the information society a boost within political rhetoric, however, is the depressed and depressing context of world recession. Analytically, the new society may be positively rather than negatively defined (as it is in *post*-industrialism). In terms of policy, entrepreneurial and innovative activity in IT may be seen as a contribution to the new society.

Although in its current form it is something of a novelty, it would be a mistake to suppose that the idea of an information society is entirely of recent origin. Alongside the analytical strands of thought about social change is another recurrent theme, technological utopianism. In Masuda, Stonier and Naisbitt we find a dream about a new kind of society which, on the one hand, appeals to empirical analysis but, on the other, is redolent with 'good society' imagery.

Technological utopianism is especially potent in the USA, where it has a long history. European utopians often made much of machines and productive advance (see Kumar, 1978) but, as Howard Segal argues, none made technological advance their panacea as did a number of American technological utopians who wrote between the 1880s and the 1930s (Segal, 1978, 1985). Electricity was the basis for their visions; then other technologies became more significant.

By the 1960s (and especially for those following the Canadian, Marshall McLuhan) the idea of an electronic utopia was fairly widespread on both sides of the Atlantic. As James Carey and John Quirk indicate, from an early stage in US history it was felt that the USA would realise 'through a marriage of nature and mechanics, an unprecedented solution to the problem of industrialisation . . . allowing us to transcend the typical evils of industrial society' (Carey and Quirk, 1970, p. 395). The ideals of decentralised democracy, community participation, an end to hierarchy and class, and of plenty for all, which suffused earlier generations of technological utopianism, reappear in the literature of information society.

Critique

Let me indicate briefly the main lines along which the information society thesis may be criticised. They are elaborated elsewhere (Lyon, 1986, 1987). I shall concentrate on the analytical aspects.

The first line of critique is carried over from the debate about post-industrialism. The leisure society, with its vast array of services, a self-expressive cultural system and greater political paticipation, does not seem to have materialised. The 'new class' of knowledge workers, whether viewed as enlightened or exploitative, is really rather incoherent, and while the university/industry connection is more significant, this hardly means that more *power* has accured to the knowledgeable. Krishan Kumar concludes that the agenda of questions for post-industrial society is painfully reminiscent of that for industrial society: alienation in the workplace, sureveillance by bureaucracy and competitive struggles for profit and power between private corporations and nation states (Kumar, 1978, p. 231).

Another line of critique which the two concepts have in common is technological determinism. The new society is the consequence of certain technological innovations. Though this is inherently false, because, among other things, technology itself is demonstrably shaped by social, cultural and economic forces (see, for example, MacKenzie and Wajcman, 1985), this aspect has telling policy implications. For instance, computerisation along prescribed lines is seen as the 'only way forward'. The slogan is 'automate or liquidate'. In fact, it is precisely our *inability* to predict the shape of society following the diffusion of IT which makes the social analytic question so interesting and important.

As we have seen, however, the information society concept takes us beyond post-industrialism. A third line of critique concerns information workers. As with post-industrialism, where some 'professionalisation' and the shift to 'white-collar' work was arguably the result of relabelling (in which 'plumber' becomes 'heating engineer', and so on), so with information society. Marc Porat and other information economy theorists have been taken to task for using the very slippery concept of 'information occupations' (doctors, on this showing, are ambiguously placed between service and information sectors). A tighter definition of information which yields clues to informative *power* is needed here (see Newman and Newman, 1985).

But a tighter definition still does not clarify things sufficiently. As Miles and Gershuny (1983, 1986) cogently argue, it is the 'march through sectors' view which is misleading. The 'march' obscures, for example, the extent to which services grow *because of growth* in manufacturing. The notion of an information sector is flawed because all sectors of the economy are becoming more information-intensive. This means that predicting the social effects of IT is all the more complex, not to say hazardous. A further benefit of this view is that *alternative* possibilities are set before us. Political choice plays a crucial role.

The importance of political and industrial choice is, in fact, played up by most economists sympathetic to the view that developments in IT could herald the start of an economic upswing along the lines suggested by Kondratiev (see, for instance, Freeman, 1982). While this is a welcome diversion from technological determinism, not all would see it as a complete alternative. For the ongoing social arrangements and processes surrounding the growth of IT already play a powerful constraining role on the growth. Military expenditure, above all, has a huge impact on what technologies are developed and where they are developed for example, (aerospace in Silicon Valley, naval defence in the Solent).

Such comments actually anticipate a fourth line of critique, already hinted at above, that the social consequences of IT are better understood as accentuating the trends of industrial capitalist society, rather than superseding it. The telecommunications-enhanced power of transnational corporations, the continuation of the Cold War by developing space weaponry, the weaker position of women within IT industries, the use of IT to monitor and control labour forces, all these and more hint at a dark side to information society.

The hard-nosed realism of such a critique contrasts with the facile futurism of some information society pundits. Social and economic analysis from these standpoints deserve a hearing. At the same time, their limitations are sometimes not dissimilar from those they set out to expose. Harry Braverman's *Labor and Monopoly Capital* (1974), for instance, which catalogues the 'degradation of works', and especially automated 'deskilling', initiated an important debate, but badly overstates the case (see Wood, 1983). Or take Fröbel *et al.* (1980) where, similarly, oversimplification misleads, this time by treating 'particular forms as the only possible outcomes of capital accumulation' (Sayer, 1986, p. 122; see also Lyon, 1986b).

The more simplistic critiques of information society also tend to be short on policy implications of their theses, either limiting themselves to purely negative critique, or advocating some form of political action which sidesteps the policy-making process.

The very existence of serious criticism of the information society thesis should give us pause. Scornful (but erroneous) references to 'Luddism', of which some newspapers, politicians and industrialists are so fond, are an inadequate response. Critique raises once more the question of the relation between social analysis and the 'good society'. Are the apparently utopian aspects of the information society susceptible to alternative interpretation? Howard Segal suggests that the contemporary significance of technological utopianism lies in the questions provoked by this paradox: technological (rather than social or cultural) changes predicted by the utopians have come into being but 'our technological society is, in most respects, far from utopian' (Segal, 1978, p. 73).

THE TWO INFORMATION SOCIETIES

In an attempt to examine the relation of the information society to public policy, I have uncovered different aspects of the concept. On the one hand are what we have referred to as its utopian overtones, which connect it with an understanding of the good society. On the other are several analytical theorems which, though inviting critique, add up to a significant agenda of sociological questions. Are we witnessing a social transformation analogous to the transition to industrial society?

May one say, then, that there are two information societies? For the purposes of this discussion it is helpful to distinguish between two understandings of the concept. This is not by any means to suggest that the evaluative aspect is somehow separable from the analytical (as I indicate below). Rather, by making this distinction, we may be clearer about what is actually meant when the term is invoked. Furthermore, the connections between the two (and thus also with public policy) may be made more explicitly and clearly.

Analytical aspects

The information society is a concept used both by those who foresee epochal change, and by those who, more modestly, refer to the radical restructuring of industrial society. Each would appeal to serious empirical analysis to make their case. But to what extent may they be said to be referring to the same thing? While it is not unlikely that the term will gain in currency as a handy concept whose sense is quickly grasped, it would be unfortunate if one version obtained a monoploy of meaning.

I have proposed that it be treated as a problematic (Lyon, 1986a, 1987). As the term is understood by Phillip Abrams, this means 'a rudimentary organisation of a field of phenomena which yields problems for investigation' (Abrams, 1982, p. xv). This rescues it from being (mis)treated as a description or theory of what has happened or is happening, and frankly acknowledges that it is an arena for debate. It is the thing to be explained rather than the explanation. But to retain its use is simultaneously to recognise the existence of a highly significant cluster of social processes which, one way or another, have an affinity with IT.

Despite the extensive criticisms that may be mounted against various interpretations of the information society concept, it does raise crucial empirical and theoretical problems (which, in turn, may have a significant bearing upon policy). Daniel Bell indicates some of these in a way which invites rebuttal (see Kumar, 1978; Webster and Robins, 1986).

Others, far more enthusiastic than he, present their analyses as apologiae for IT. The resultant danger here, as William Melody, says, is that critique of information society literature be 'characterised more as a direct response to the promotional claims, rather than an attempt to examine rigorously probable implications [of IT] in the real world' (Melody, 1985, p. 267).

Such rigorous empirical investigation may, of course, spark off or support alternative theoretical explorations as well. When sociological analysis questions the appropriateness and adequacy of its own time-honoured concepts — industrial, capitalist — it would be unsurprising to discover new concepts being proposed. Perhaps, for example, social and economic power is becoming less directly associated with the mode of production, and more with what has been termed the 'mode of information'? (Poster, 1984, 1987).

Such issues would all be fair game within the information society problematic. Also essential to such a problematic, in my view, would be the debate over technological determinism and its converse, the social shaping of technology, the interplay between regional and global factors, the social and political implications of the technical convergence between computers and telecommunications, and the interface between social science and public policy.

Evaluative aspects

Let me return to Segal's paradox. Contrary to the utopian predictions, he says, only the technical changes have come about, not the social and cultural changes. Indeed, American technological society is 'far from utopian'. The paradox is explicable, however. A vision of the desirable society may function in more than one way. The technological society may have both utopian *and* ideological aspects.

Seen as a world in which convenience and release from drudgery are augmented, whether by telephones, automatic cars, or computerised machine tools, the utopian aspects are patent (and enthusiasm for them may be shared by the political left and right, see, for example, Gorz, 1982). But the same world may also be viewed as the locus for State surveillance (phone tapping) and capitalist control (deskilling and the wresting of responsibility from workers). In this account, the ideological aspects surface; the purportedly liberating technology actually enlarges the power of the dominant.

Technological potential is not social destiny. It is a mistake to move from the individual and personal benefits of specific technological objects — word processors for journalists and secretaries, or computerised aids for the disabled — to suppose that the overall cumulative social impacts of automated production or the electronic office will be equally benign. IT does offer great potential for decentralisation of business and administration (which could be read as a desirable, even utopian goal), but whether or not that occurs depends on a complex range of factors as well as technical capacity. So those who see, or believe, there ought to be utopian aspects within the information society concept are not necessarily mistaken. Rather, they would be mistaken if they assumed that the existence of the technology enlarged the chance of realising that utopia.

To qualify as utopia at all, a view of the good society must at least present a radical alternative to that society, stand as a judgement upon present society, and offer a means of achieving its aims. It is not at all clear that the utopian aspects of the information society meet those criteria. Indeed, the information society may be read with at least equal plausibility as serving the status quo.

Anthony Giddens has suggested that ideological aspects are present when sectional interests are presented as universal, when contradictions are denied or transmuted, and when the present is made to appear as the 'natural' state of affairs (Giddens, 1979, pp. 193-5). At a time when technology policy is granted higher status than employment policy, when the 'new-style management' characteristic of some high-tech companies is declared to represent the end of hierarchy and class conflict, and when computerisation is held out as the 'next stage' of technological progress, it would appear that information society indeed qualifies as having ideological aspects.

Krishan Kumar (1978, p. 327) deplores the post-industrialist attempt to foreclose the future. He warns that it would be disastrous in practice to confront the future with a vision of society which is thought of as a bigger and more efficient version of the present. Yet this is what some information society fututists seem to press for; Bob Goudzwaard uses the phrase 'closed' or 'tunnel society' (Goudzwaard, 1979 p. 183). He recalls John Maynard Keynes's statement (1932, p. 372) that 'Avarice and usury and precaution must be our gods for a little longer still. For only they can lead us out of the tunnel of economic necessity into daylight.' A closed society is one in which everything contributes to the smooth advance towards the light. Goudzwaard says the lights shine forever *in the future*, but function to keep everything and everyone in the tunnel on the move.

Goudzwaard rightly observes that in societies which exhibit such relative closedness, meaning and value tend to be accorded only to those features and factors which contribute to advance within the tunnel. Perhaps that is an exaggeratedly bleak way of looking at the role of the information society in public policy, but it seems to ring bells at least regarding industrial location and educational innovation. Such an outlook leaves precious little space for conceiving genuine alternatives to the social conditions and directions of the present.

As a description or theory, the information society concept is flawed. But as a problematic which alerts us to some of the most pressing sociological questions of our day, it is vital. As a utopia it is, at best, inadequate. At worst, its ideological aspects are more potent than its utopian ones. Some would see it as a (possibly disastrous) means of maintaining the status quo, which could exacerbate rather than alleviate the contradictions of industrial capitalsm. All of which, if true, makes the need for alternative conceptions of the good society all the more apparent. What then are the implications of this for social analysis and public policy related to IT?

IMPLICATIONS FOR POLICY

The claim that we are entering the information society has important policy implications. If that claim is in some way mistaken or inadequate it is surely an appropriate task for social analysts to draw attention to this and to suggest modifications or alternatives.

In his book *Social Science and Public Policy (1976)*, Martin Rein suggests that social science is a form of 'story-telling', dependent upon analogy, metaphor, and so on. The story-telling gives an interpretation of a complex pattern of events which, in turn, has normative implications for action (p. 268). The social analyst will attempt to refine and apply the story and to test the validity of other stories.

The information society concept is part of one such story. It depends upon analogy (with the familiar image of industrial society) and metaphor (social activities being predominantly bound up with information and its related technological objects, like computers). And it is a story which is still being told. Indeed, it is intended to contribute to the plot, because it is about what society is becoming.

However, in the version associated with Daniel Bell which, it must be said, attracts considerable respect among policy-makers, the information society story takes the form of a 'social forecast'. In this story, what is observable appears as more or less inevitable trends which, it turns out, are also desirable. John Goldthorpe was one of the first to expose this kind of story as one which leaves little room for moral dissent (Goldthorpe. 1971). It is 'technocratic historicism', whose politics are gradualism and moderation.

Since Goldthorpe was writing, however, hopes for the information society have become an important aspect of New Right politics. Michael Goldhaber lists three particular aspirations associated with IT (American ones, but equally applicable elsewhere): to re-establish economic pre-eminence; to limit or crush the power of organised labour; and to restore military supremacy to the USA (Goldhaber, 1986, pp. 108–9). This once more highlights the fact that the 'information society' is a far from neutral concept (and is not intended to imply that the political left currently offers credible alternative IT policies).

Social analysis and policy
The validity of the received 'information society story' has been tested in several ways, and found wanting. Nonetheless, as a problematic which alerts us to crucial social trends (and maybe transformations) it may still have a significant policy-related role.

One of the main difficulties with the information society concept is that by focusing all attention on what is new (especially the technical revolutions represented by computer 'generations', concern is deflected from the major continuities of industrial capitalist society). The traditional divisions between the sexes, for instance, appear to be perpetuated within societies adopting new technology. The disadvantaged position of minority groups, likewise, appears to be as stubbornly evident as ever. Regional development within nations, and between north and south, remains highly uneven, a situation which is, if anything, worsening.

Take another example. Whatever the long-term prospects for employment, the overwhelming evidence from several societies is that in the medium term, at least, the introduction of new technology is unlikely to offset anything like the numbers of people displaced from more traditional industries. In policy terms this does not necessarily demand a switch from the quest of technological advance, but rather the frank acknowledgement that such policies on their own hold out no hope for those whose energies are currently flagging. In short, much of the political agenda remains relatively unchanged.

On the other hand, the virtue of the information society concept is precisely that it makes us ask questions about what is new in our world. Those involved in policy debate and implementation should be aware of the various impacts of IT which are already making themselves felt. The augmentation of deskilling, the demise of the middle manager, and the effects of electronic funds transfer are all fairly obvious areas for dialogue between social analysis and public policy-making.

More elusive, perhaps, but potentially very significant, are the social and cultural implications of highly malleable data, the vulnerability as well as the threat, of centralised computer systems (especially those which are State-owned), and the effects on human sociality of increased interaction with machines. This has implications for education policy, if nothing else. Rather than thinking simply (and simplistically) of how to help young people 'fit into' a society in which IT is implicated in an ever-growing proportion of social and economic exchanges, should we not consider how to enable the next generation to confront these wider issues?

Social analysis best contributes to policy-making by showing that, whether the restructuring of industrial society warrants the designation 'information society' or not, neither the importance of the continuing trends nor the social changes related to IT should be minimised.

The good society and policy

The supposed 'facts' about information society should not be allowed to determine policy. Some of the predictions made by information society theorists — greater participation, renewed community, and so on — may well resound with social values about which one could find considerable consenus. The problem is not that the analysis used for policy reflects some vision or world view (for all such analyses do that), it is that it is a sort of tunnel vision. This has two major effects.

Firstly, it concentrates upon information (and its cognate microelectronics-based technologies) as if this were the good, or the provider of good. When put so baldly, the idea that information could be a good or an end in itself is palpably wrong. And yet the way in which IT is enthusiastically grasped by so many institutions and organisations before any clear objectives for its use have been formulated, and the ways in which government policy promotes automation suggest that this statement is implicitly correct.

Secondly, this tunnel vision tends to exclude consideration of alternatives. Computers arrived 'just in time' to help administrators cope with paperwork in bureaucracies, or to avoid confrontation with labour unions, or to eradicate the possibility of nuclear war. Automation is often viewed as having the necessary, but unfortunate, side effect of deskilling (but see, for example, Rosenbrock, 1984). Such failures to conceive of alternatives (whether bureaucratic reform, new technology agreements, a nuclear freeze or skills retention) create a climate in which dissent is increasingly difficult.

In the later 1980s it is only social movements (such as environmentalists and ecology groups, plus perhaps feminists) whose voices are heard questioning policies which appear to uphold the status quo. At the same time, paradoxically, efforts to impose new priorities upon the educational system may also serve to enliven the debate over appropriate social and economic goals. But who will contribute to that debate? In conclusion, let me indicate three possible sources, none of which, let it be said, are technophobic. All would pursue policies which involved the positive development of IT.

Firstly, some of the theorists mentioned previously already contribute to that debate. Miles and Gershuny, for instance, insist that IT should not be seen simply in relation to old systems and processes, but in terms of its possible contribution to a new socio-technical system. In their policy discussion they stress such things as the urgent need for an adequate telecommunications infrastructure as a prerequisite to further social and technical innovation.

Secondly, a number of recent writings attempt to place technological development in a social and political context, and to argue that specific social values should help determine what is appropriate technology (for example, Burns, 1984). Goldhaber calls this 'reinventing technology as a social system so that it can better meet our needs' (1986, p. 123). He urges a restatement of 'democratic values' which would redirect technology, and proposes a number of specific policies to facilitate their realisation. Job design and community technology are two such policies.

Thirdly, a place should be made for a religious approach to questions of technology and society. Philosopher Hans Jonas highlights the ethical issues thrown up by today's technology which both unites the globe and threatens its very existence in unprecedented ways. He pinpoints the irony that just when ethical guidance is required on such a scale, the same Western rationality cuts itself off from the acient sources of wisdom which could help (Jonas, 1984). Today, the Christian notion of stewardship in economic life is antithetical to conventional economic thought which places such store on new technology (see Monsma *et al.*, 1986). Yet would such an economic and technological outlook, whose concerns are care for one's neighbour and for the earth, justice and community, be so out of place?

BIBLIOGRAPHY

Abrams, P. (1982), *Historical Sociology*, Open Books, Shepton Mallet.
Bell, D. (1973), *The Coming of Post-Industrial Society*, Penguin, Harmondsworth.

Bell, D. (1980), 'The social framework of the information society', in Forester, T. (ed.), *The Microelectronic Revolution*, Blackwell, Oxford.
Beresford, P. (1986), 'The Solent fast lane to the future', *Sunday Times*, 25 May, p. 56.
Bessant, J., Guy, K., Mikes, I., and Rush, H. (1985), *IT Futures: What Current Forecasting Literature says about the Social Impact of Information Technology*, NEDC, London.
Bjorn-Anderson, N. (1982), *The Information Society: for richer, for poorer*, North-Holland, Amsterdam and London.
Braverman, H. (1974), *Labour and Monopoly Capital*, Monthly Review Press, New York.
Burns, A. (1984), *The Microchip: Appropriate or Inappropriate Technology?*, Horwood-Ellis, Winchester.
Carey, J., and Quirk, J. (1970), *The American Scholar, 39* (2), pp. 219–41; *39* (3), pp. 395–424.
CERI (1986), *New Information Technologies: a Challenge for Education*, OECD, Paris.
Cordell, A. (1985), *The Uneasy Eighties: the Transition to an Information Society*, Science Council of Canada, Ottawa.
The Development of Higher Education into the 1990s (1985), HMSO, Cmnd. 9524, May.
DTI (1982), *Information Technology: the Age of Electronic Information*, Department of Trade and Industry, London.
Dutton, P., Nicholls, P., and Prestt, B. (1984), *All Change*, Microelectronics Education Programme/National Extension College.
Edgar, P., and Rahim, Syed (eds) (1983), *Communication Policy in Developed Countries*, Kegan Paul International, London and Boston.
Freeman, C., Clarke, J., and Soete, L. (1982), *The Economics of Unemployment and Technological Innovation*, Frances Pinter, London.
Fröbel, F., Heinrichs, J., and Kreye, O. (1980), *The New International Division of Labour*, Cambridge University Press.
Gershuny, J., and Miles, I. (1983), *The New Service Economy*, Frances Pinter, London.
Giddens, A (1979), *Central Problems in Social Theory*, Macmillan, London.
Goldhaber, M. (1986), *Reinventing Technology: Policies for Democratic Values*, Routledge & Kegan Paul, London and Boston.
Goldthorpe, J. (1971), 'Reflections on the recrudescence of hisoricism and the future of futurology', *Archives of European Sociology, XII*.
Gorz, A. (1982), *Farewell to the Working Class*, Pluto, London.
Goudzwaard, B. (1979), *Capitalism and Progress*, Wedge, Toronto and Eerdmans, Grand Rapids.
Jonas, H. (1984), *The Imperative of Responsibility*, University of Chicago Press.
Keynes, J. M., (1932), 'Economic possibilities for our grandchildren,' in *Essays in Persuasion*, Harcourt Brace and Co., New York.
Kumar, K. (1978), *Prophecy and Progress*, Penguin, Harmondsworth.
Larsen, J., and Rogers, A. (1984), *Silicon Valley Fever*, Allen & Unwin, London, and Basic Books, New York.
Lyon, D. (1986a), 'From post-industrialism to information society: a new social transformation?', *Sociology, 20* (4), pp. 111–22.
Lyon, D. (1986b),'Marxist misgivings about the information society: help or hindrance in facing the future?', in Jain, A., and Matejko, A., *A Critique of Marxist and Non-Marxist Thought*, Praeger, New York.

Lyon, D. (1987) ' Information technology and information society: a reply to Fincham', *Sociology*, 21 (3), pp. 467-8.
Lyon, D. (1988), *The Information Society: Issues and Illusions*, Polity Press, Cambridge.
Machlup, F. (1980), *The Production and Distribution of Knowledge in the USA*, Princeton.
Mackenzie, D., asnd Wajcman, J. (eds) (1985), *The Social Shaping of Technology*, Open University Press, Milton Keynes.
Masuda, Y. (1971), *The plan for information society: a national goal toward the year 2000*, Japan Computer Usage Development Institute, Tokyo.
Masuda, Y. (1982), *Information Society as Post-industrial Society*, World Futures Society, Bethesda, Md.
Melody, W. (1985), Editorial, *Media, Culture and Society*, 7, pp. 267-70.
Miles, I., and Gershuny, J. (1986), 'The social economics of IT,' in Ferguson, M. (ed.), *New Communication Technology and the Public Interest*, Sage, London.
Monsma, S. (ed.) (1986), *Responsible Technology*, Eerdmans, Grand Rapids.
Naisbitt, J. (1984), *Megatrends*, Warner Books, New York.
Newman, J., and Newman, R. (1985), 'Information work: the new divorce?', *British Journal of Sociology*, *XXXVI* (4), pp. 497-515.
Nora, S., and Minc, A. (1980), *The Computerisation of Society*, MIT Press, Cambridge, Mass.
Porat, M. (1977), *The Information Ecomony: Definition and Measurement*, US Dept. of Commerce, Washington.
Poster, M. (1988) ,*The Mode of Information*, Polity Press, Cambridge.
Poster, M. (1984), *Foucault, Marxism and History: From Mode of Production to Mode of Information*, Polity Press, Cambridge.
Rein, M. (1976), *Social Science and Public Policy*, Penguin, Harmondsworth.
Robins, K., and Webster, F. (1985), Higher education, high technology, and high rhetoric, in Solomonides, T., and Levidow, L. (eds), *Compulsive Technology*, Free Association Books, London.
Rosenbrock, H. (1984), 'Designing automated systems: must skills be lost?', in Marstrand, P. (ed.), *New Technology and Future of Work and Skills*, Frances Pinter, London.
Sayer, A. (1986), 'Industrial location on a world scale: the case of the semiconductor industry', in Scott, A., and Storper, M. (eds), *Production, Work, Territory*, Allen & Unwin, Boston.
Science Council of Canada (1982), *Planning Now for the Information Society: Tomorrow is too late*, Ministry of Supply, Ottawa.
Segal, H. (1978), 'American visions of technological utopia', *Markham Review*,7.
Segal, H. p. (1985), *Technological Utopianism in American Culture*, University of Chicago Press, Chicago.
Stonier, T. (1983), *The Wealth of Information*, Thames Methuen, London.
Taylor, T. (1983), 'High technology industry and the development of science parks', in *Built Environment*, 9 (1) (repr. in Markusen, A., and Hall, P. (eds) (1985), *Silicon Landscapes*, Allen & Unwin, London).
Toffler, A. (1980), *The Third Wave*, Pan, London.
Tomforde, A. (1986), 'German "Silicon Valley" takes root in Black Forest', *Guardian*, 3 January.

Tucker, M. (1985), 'Computers in schools: what revolution?', *Journal of Communications*, *35* (4), pp. 12–23.
Webster, F., and Robins, K. (1986), *Information Technology: a Luddite Analysis*, Ablex, Norwood, New Jersey.
Wood, S. (ed.) (1983), *The Degradation of Work?*, Heinemann, London.
Woronoff, J. (1985), 'Japan and the 21st century', *Oriental Economist*, September, pp. 31–3.

Internationalisation and the production of technology and information

HOWARD WILLIAMS
Centre for Urban and Regional Development Studies
University of Newcastle upon Tyne

OVERVIEW

The purpose of this chapter is to explore some of the recent developments in Information technology (IT) both in terms of IT production industries and the emergence of information markets. It is argued that developments within the IT sector are taking place in an international context and, as such, pose major threats to IT policy-making and implementation in a national setting. Further, it is argued that the acceptance by policy-makers of the technologists' paradigm as the legitimate structure within which to conceive and develop IT policy is misplaced.

The methodological foundations of this chapter are essentially Schumpeterian. It is argued that for policy-makers this theoretical framework offers an understanding of IT that points up implications of both the technology and the development of new economic activities, that is, the opportunities and threats created by trade in information.

RESEARCH ISSUES

From a position of relative strength in the late 1950s and early 1960s, the IT industry within Europe has been reduced to a mere shadow of its former self. The initiative once held in terms of the development of the technology has been lost to Japanese and American companies. Further, and partially as a result of the relative decline in Europe's technological base, there has been an abject failure of European companies to penetrate successfully internationally competitive markets for IT products and services. There have been several studies[1] which have attempted to assess the impacts of the demise of Europe's IT industry, all of which make depressing reading, particularly in terms of lost employment and wealth-creating opportunities. What is common amongst these studies is their conclusion that technological regeneration is the route to the salvation of the European IT sector. Thus, across Europe there has been a proliferation of technology-based policies, for example, Alvey in the UK and, on a European level, ESPRIT. The concern of these policies is not just that European companies have a low market share, which is itself the reflection of a myriad of problems, it is more that European companies are becoming unable to trade in IT markets on the basis of in-house developed products and services. The argument is that control of the technology is vital to the survival of IT production companies.

The interaction of changing technology, customer requirements, and international competition has reduced product life cycles and increased the risk associated with research and development. In so doing these forces of change necessitate responses from IT firms that are both broader in their scope (international) and more timely (immediate) than those fostered by the technology-driven policy initiatives sponsored by European governments. The nature of these corporate responses, as individual companies strive to maintain or enhance their competitive advantage, raises profound problems for national governments, particularly in terms of the control of the technological base and high-technology trade flows.

With respect to high-technology trade, the responses that are being implemented by European companies create structure which militate against the efficacy of policies which are designed and implemented nationally. For example, the incorporation of high-technology products into the products of national companies means that trade restrictions initiated in response to deteriorating trade balances are self-defeating. Furthermore, these newly created corporate structures, whilst giving immediate access to a vital technology, do not necessarily provide long-term guarantees.[2] In addition, 'conduits' are created which permit the relatively easy export of gains from technology orientated IT policies which are, by and large, financed and implemented nationally.

Another set of policy issues arises because the application of IT has created structures which allow, even necessitate, trade in information. The technology has created the necessary, although not sufficient, conditions for the commodification of information and the growth of the network marketplace.[3] Changes are, however, required in socio-economic, regulatory, and legal frameworks to ensure the development of this network marketplace and the emergence of the information economy.

THEORETICAL FRAMEWORKS

The theoretical foundations of this paper are essentially Schumpeterian but include recent developments in long-wave theory. It is argued that the Schumpeterian view is the most pertinent to the study of IT because of its emphasis upon the *carriers* of a new technological paradigm and the *transformation* of existing products and processes. In the first instance, digital electronic technology has led to the creation of new industrial sectors (for example, semiconductors). Second, the technology is having a profound effect upon the nature of economic activity across all sectors, particularly in terms of the creation of a myriad of economic opportunities centred upon information as an economic resource.

The basic tenet of the Schumpeterian theory of economic growth is that growth is dependent upon the ability and initiative of entrepreneurs to realise opportunities for new investment; growth and employment drawing upon the discoveries of scientists and innovators. The emphasis is on autonomous investment embodying new technical innovation. In consequence, the framework for economic growth can be perceived as a process of resource allocation *between* industries. Economic growth is not merely accompanied by fast-growing new industries, it is dependent upon such industries and the transformation of methods of production in traditional industries.

After 1945, the synergy between a new technological paradigm and existing institutions resulted in sustained economic growth in those sectors that exploited low-cost energy and energy-intensive materials (for example, organic chemicals). Corporate conventional wisdom was equated with the large-scale mass production of energy-intensive standardised products. The new technological paradigm is based upon the low costs of storing, processing and communicating information. It is the fundamental technologies of active components, data processing, telecommunications and software that constitute the kernel of IT, and form the basis of a new wave of economic activity.[4]

STRUCTURAL CHANGES IN THE IT PRODUCTION SECTOR

The purpose of this section is to illustrate just three areas of change that are shaping the development of the IT production industry, the carriers of the new technological paradigm. The three areas are strategic alliances, manufacturing systems and labour markets. The first two areas illustrate the way in which the industry is becoming global in its perspective, developing structures and strategies that threaten to eclipse national jurisdiction in key policy areas, such as, competition, trade and technology. The third area highlights the differential nature of job opportunities within the industry by occupation category and the relative stability of total employment.

Strategic alliances

The uncertainties that exist within the IT sector, both in terms of markets and technology, have forced organisations and companies to review the nature of their business and their response to an internationally competitive environment. Increasingly, companies are developing global product strategies which attempt to satisfy the conflicting objectives of undifferentiated global components and subassemblies, and highly differentiated products for numerous end markets, defined both functionally and geographically. This trend can be interpreted as an attempt to shift the barriers to entry away from technology and towards both the scale and scope of production and market distribution. Further, this phenomenon can be explained as an attempt to reduce the instability in volatile markets created by the interaction of changing consumer demands and technology. As a consequence of this interaction between consumers and technology, the perceived period of the product life cycle in which profits can be expected to be earned to recover development costs is severely circumscribed and often no more than three years. Thus, the volumes needed to cover escalating design, development, production and marketing costs, and to sustain the profitability of the company have grown enormously. However, the scale of national markets, particularly within Europe, are insufficient to meet this volume/time constraint and *international* sales have, therefore, become a prerequisite to success. In consequence there has been considerable investment in process automation which has produced the economies of scale necessary to operate internationally. These economies of sale by their nature are not divisible. For complex multinational companies this has meant production establishments have become increasingly focused on a particular 'mission', often with

Table 3.1. Strategic alliances

	Equity-based	Non-equity-based
Exchange of resources	Equity investments ties with spin-offs	Cross-licensing technology–marketing/ manufacturing exchanges Consumer–supplier relations
Joint development	Consortia joint ventures	Consortia joint development of products or technologies

Source: Gorbis (1985).

sole global responsibility for that activity. For example, the IBM facility at Winchester has been designated sole supplier for a new generation of compact memory devices for the system 38 medium-scale computers.[5] For smaller companies the problems are more acute and this had led to reviews of in-house activity.

In effect, companies are being forced to assemble both technologically advanced products with a limited life cycle and secure timely volume sales in a multitude of geographically disparate markets. This dual problem has invoked an almost standard response of establishing strategic alliances. That is to say an international *confederation*, not conglomeration, of companies held together primarily through the exchange of market access and technology. Strategic alliances do not involve acquisitions or mergers, although they may involve equity-based agreements. Table 3.1 illustrates the types of strategic alliances that can occur.

For individual companies membership of a strategic alliance confers substantial benefits, although the nature of the organisation may change to reflect the overall needs of the alliance. At one extreme, a company may well be able to abandon manufacturing and all associated products and process development, and concentrate on being no more than an entry point into a particular market. Thus, a national IT company could divest its manufacturing capabilities and become no more than a distributor or system integrator of another company's products. Alternatively, a company could become an internationally competitive supplier of a particular product and/or technology, although it would still provide a comprehensive product range through the alliance. The potential outcomes of an alliance are essentially dependent upon the relative *international* competitiveness of its constituents, for, in the end, activity is allocated to the maximum competitive benefit of the alliance.

A partial, and inevitably outdated, analysis of the strategic groupings centred upon major European companies is given in figure 3.1. What is evident is the complex web of international alliances that supports a multitude of companies, and the existence of key companies that form 'nodes' in these networks. Further, competitors are often linked via these networks.

Through an analysis of the nature of individual alliances an assessment can be made of the comparative technological strengths of national industries. What emerges from such an analysis is that European–Japanese or European–American alliances essentially involve access to European markets in exchange for technology from the non-European partner. It is exceptional for the technological flow to be from Europe to either the USA or Japan. This is a reflection of the technological lag that exists within Europe. Moreover, it means that for European companies, access to the relatively large markets in the USA and Japan is dependent upon acquisition, which is inherently a high-risk strategy (for example, Siemens in the USA). Further, in the case of some European companies, the exchange of market access for technology has led to a reduction in the indigenous research and development (Rand D) effort to a level from which it is, in aggregate, both expensive and time-consuming to recover. As such, strategic alliances pose fundamental questions about the ability to maintain a credible national presence in leading edge technologies and may be detrimental to the long-term viability of Europe's IT industries.

The deterioration of trade balances in IT products and services is a major and growing problem for many governments. For example, in the UK the IT trade deficit (excluding software) in 1985 was in the order of £1·7 billion (US) and ACARD (1986) have projected a £2 billion (US) deficit in software alone by the early 1990s. It is a problem that is exacerbated by strategic alliances, for they create a quasi-institutional structure for imports. Imports are not only an integral part of a domestic company's product range, but form part of a broader inter-corporate trade of intentions and expectations upon which long-term growth is dependent. Thus, whilst the substitution of specific imports is possible, the broader based exchanges that occur within an alliance, and which are of such strategic importance, are not. As a result, a traditional trade policy response to a deficit based upon restrictions is fraught with new complexities.

In short, strategic alliances are corporate responses to an increas-

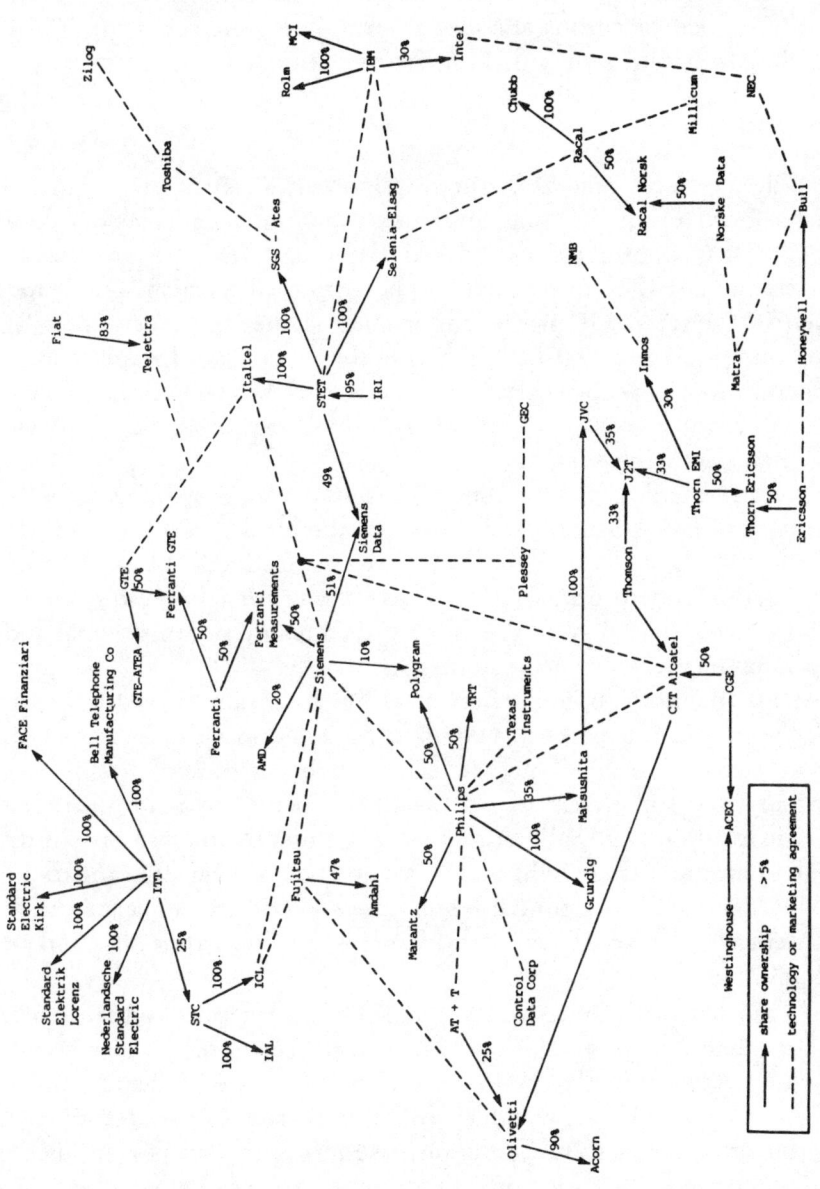

The production of technology and information 49

FIG 3.1. Summary of some ownership linkages and technology and/or marketing agreements between IT producers, as at August 1985 (Note: A number of these linkages have changed substantially)

ingly uncertain and internationally competitive environment. Further, strategic alliances are allowing a subtle restructuring of IT industry on a global basis based upon the exchange of markets for technology. The integration of corporations at a global level, however, raises questions about the efficacy of policy making at the national level.

Manufacturing systems
In parallel, yet still related to the development of strategic alliances, there has been a radical change in the nature of *input* linkages between firms. These changes are encapsulated in new and flexible manufacturing systems and the consequent impacts upon the organisation and location of activity. Of prime importance is the implementation of production strategies that both increase the flexibility of manufacturing operations and reduce costs. As a result there has been a rapid move in recent years to Just-in-Time (JIT)[6] and away from Just-in-Case (JIC) manufacturing systems.

JIT is a method of production organisation that allows the delivery of product to the consumer directly from the production line and not from a stock of pre-made (anticipated orders) products. Thus, the rate of production is determined by the current level of sales, and production becomes subservient to the market. As a result, organisational and operational changes are necessitated.

Perhaps the most obvious effect of JIT is the dramatic reduction in stock levels and the emphasis upon suppliers and subcontractors to deliver 'Just-in-Time'. Thus, it has often been argued that JIT is essentially a stockholding externalisation process[7] with implications upon the location of suppliers; that is, they must be in close proximity to main manufacturing facilities.[8] It is evident, however, that the move to JIT reflects far more fundamental issues which are concerned with the internalisation of IT markets than merely the externalisation of stockholdings.

Concomitant with the introduction of JIT, companies redefine their in-house manufacturing and reallocate resources to only those activities which are perceived to be major sources of value added and capable of sustained growth. The analysis of value added is extended to each potential supplier so that each enterprise in the system is responsible for that element in which it can achieve greatest value added. In consequence, a process of aggregating *international* competitive advantage is formalised into the total production system. Those activities which fall outside these criteria are externalised, sometimes by spinning them off into independent firms. The process of externalisation is, however, ameliorated by a number of factors, including both internal corporate considerations, and the external social and political environment. In the latter case, for example, where redundancies cannot freely be made, the introduction of JIT may result in the internalisation of previous subcontracted tasks (for example, the telecommunications equipment industry in Southern Italy).

In exchange for a commitment to support a JIT manufacturing system, suppliers are able to reduce some of the risks of being in business whilst maintaining flexibility. Not only do primary manufacturers place volume orders at economic prices, they also provide a substantial input into all aspects of the business, including process technology (often including the provision of the machine tools), management development, and forewarning of product development plans. Thus, enterprises within a JIT system become mutually supportive and responsive to the needs of volatile markets.

Inevitably, to maintain production within a JIT system, meticulous attention must be paid to quality. In fact, JIT is based upon suppliers having capability to meet orders both in terms of time and quality. In the semiconductor industry the target is fault-free product, and already it is becoming common to measure quality in terms of parts per billion. Further, the stock held of some consumables is down to just several *hours* of production, with the plant dependent on multiple daily deliveries; whilst, in other cases, particularly for 'tools' (for example, pumps), no stock is held at all. These expectations of timeliness and quality of output are reflected throughout the system, and failure to meet delivery schedules (both for time and quality) result in *no* business not reduced business. If rejection does not occur then the re-entry costs faced by a firm are substantial, if not insurmountable.

The implementation of JIT alters the relationship between contractor and client from one primarily based upon price to one based upon a mutual understanding of long-term business needs. This can pose severe problems of adaptation for suppliers. These problems are illustrated by the difficulties which Brother, a Japanese-owned office equipment manufacturer, has had in identifying suitable subcontractors to satisfy the needs of their branch plant in South Wales.[9] The concern of Brother is that without appropriate suppliers the market reputation of their product is put at risk and, as a result, the rationale for their investment in Europe is challenged.

The extent to which the end 'manufacturer' maintains *control* over the 'intelligence' within the product is central to assessing whether or not the consequences of JIT can be perceived as beneficial. The 'intelligence' within a product can be seen as consisting of a number of factors. Firstly, there are the enabling technologies behind various subassemblies (for example, semiconductor technology). Secondly, there is the 'intelligence': that is, direct knowledge of customers and their future needs. Control over these factors determines for example product design. Thirdly, there is market or business intelligence, that is the extent to which a supplier is able to invest independently in ventures that broaden the trading base of the company or rely on the client for such information. Inevitably, JIT changes the distribution of 'intelligence' and, as such, changes the nature of the dependency between suppliers. A supplier, however, internationally competitive at manufacturing a component or subassembly, remains vulnerable if the information upon which the development of its business is based, is exclusively provided by the end manufacturer in the JIT system. In effect, the viability of such suppliers is no longer subject solely to market pressures, but is dependent upon a range of other factors.

In short, JIT is a manufacturing system that reconfigures the nature of input linkages and consequent relations between firms. The conventional notion of trading by price alone is obsolete. Similar to strategic alliances, JIT is a process of integration of individual companies into internationally competitive manufacturing groupings. The result, however, is that the entire manufacturing system is controlled by the end 'manufacturer' because of its authority over final product design and access to markets. The quasi-institutional agreements implemented between companies across national boundaries pose complex questions for policies developed and implemented in national jurisdictions.

Labour markets

From a policy perspective, one of the main interests in the IT production sector has been its potential for providing jobs — both to replace those lost by declining 'sunset' industries and to provide new opportunities in still industrialising regions. In spite of the impressive *output* growth in the IT sectors, their ability to provide *net* new jobs must be questioned. In many of the IT sectors (such as components, computers and telecommunications) very substantial productivity improvements have been made, due to both product and process innovations. In the UK, for example, the volume of output from the electronic computer industry doubled between 1971 and 1978 while employment contracted by 10 percent. The term 'jobless growth'[10] has been used to describe the situation that prevailed in the electronics sector, but it is perhaps now more accurately described as job-loss growth.[11]

The skill structures of the IT industries depart substantially from those which prevail in most other manufacturing industries. Labour requirements are becoming polarised between a small, but relatively rapidly growing, segment of highly qualified labour (scientists, technicians, managers) and a large, but declining, unskilled, semi-skilled work-force engaged in assembly. This trend towards a bifurcated work-force has resulted in skilled manual labour becoming under-represented in the IT production sector.

The concept of a bifurcated work-force, however, disguises the extent to which highly qualified scientific and technical staff are becoming integrated into production at the expense of traditional skilled and semi-skilled labour, and is a reflection of both increased process automation and changing sources of value-added. For example, in the software sector the skill profile is dominated by those who are highly educated and professionally trained. One of the possible explanations of this need for such highly skilled people is in the nature of the production process itself. Although considerable effort has been devoted to the development of production tools, it is still difficult to separate the various stages of software production. However, as production tools become available it can reasonably be expected that the production process will be divided, and this will result in the functional and spatial division of labour. In the semiconductor sector, employees are a major source of contamination that reduces the yield of the production process. Therefore, the trend is to automate processes and this reduces demand for employees overall, but in particular for skilled and semi-skilled employees. Further, increasing degrees of automation necessitate the employment of highly skilled and educated employees in the production process which puts further pressure upon employment opportunities for semi-skilled workers. By contrast, in the telecommunications sector changing sources of value added have moved the production environment from the factory floor and the fabrication of electro-mechanical switches to the office, and the writing of software and design of semiconductors and specialised circuits.

However, not only is the skill profile of the industry changing, but the importance attached to skill compared with other attributes is declining. Increasingly, companies are becoming concerned with 'social' skills, in particular adaptability, flexibility and commercial awareness. The quasi-institutional structures discussed above (for example, JIT) that enhance flexibility and responsiveness are predicated upon a highly skilled and flexible work-force. Therefore, IT companies have generally adopted thorough recruitment process in which it is explicitly recognised that possession of technical skills is no longer a necessary and sufficient condition to achieving employment. It is not uncommon for applicants to be subjected to extensive psychological initiative and character tests before any assessment of their 'skills'.

In parallel with developments in the technical and social skill profile of the work-force, major IT companies have pioneered 'progressive' employment policies designed to ensure the flexibility of the organisation and to maintain and enhance employees' job satisfaction. This latter point is significant for, within many segments of the IT sector, people are the key resource, even in manufacturing activities and, compares with other sectors, the movement of employees between firms, is accepted as an industry norm. The loss of key staff can be damaging and in competitive labour markets replacement of staff is, at the minimum, time consuming and expensive.

The corner-stone of these new employment practices is the individualisation of employer and employee relations. For individuals these new employment practices mean that there are no salary scales and grades. The basis of pay is upon an individual's contribution to the firm and is not related to the direct output of the employee. One of the main advantages of this method of payment is that the flexibility of employees is increased, for their perceptions of pay are not related to a specific task. The process, however, necessitates a formalised staff appraisal system that is seen to be open, explicit and fair. Also there is a tendency towards formal and *direct* communications between the levels of the firm's hierarchy on all aspects of the business. One of the best examples of these new employment practices is Texas Instruments where they have managed to achieve the individualisation of substantially all employee and employer relationships in the UK.

Although not a complete explanation, new employment practices are contributing to the absence of any strong trade union presence within the industry. On one level the procedures adopted by firms over pay negotiation and communication remove one of the most tangible benefits of belonging to a trades union. But perhaps more fundamentally, the changing composition of the work-force is affecting the 'appreciative setting' in which trades unions have to operate. As recently observed by a leading trades unionist in the UK, 'IBM actually owns the most sophisticated and far-sighted personnel policy of any company which I have knowledge . . . Unless that point is understood, all attempts to secure trade union recognition at IBM will fail because the staff will not join.[12]'

The notion of *skill shortage* in the IT sector has been in the public domain for a number of years and it has been argued that the shortage of skilled employees is inhibiting the development of the sector in Europe.[13] However, a complex and often conflicting picture emerged from research into the sector.[14] It was in only a relatively few cases that companies identified skill shortages as a fundamental constraint under which they operated. In those companies where problems associated with skill shortage are percieved to be insignificant, there was evidence that they had taken full cognisance of the fact that individuals are the key resource. Thus, considerable attention was paid to manpower planning, project management and training. These companies were interpreting changes in the market into possible employment effects and planning their recruitment and training accordingly. In consequence, they tended to be in a position to resource projects with appropriately trained employees rather than having to recruit. It appeared that where skill shortages did exist the companies had an expectation that the local labour market should be able to provide appropriately trained individuals as and when required. The question is to what extent is this a reasonable expectation of the performance of local labour markets?

In the more general context of labour markets, changes in the skill profile of employees have profound influences upon the ability of companies to operate effectively in certain types of labour markets. In the past the requirement for skilled and unskilled *manual* labour was an overriding consideration, and the availability and quality of such labour influenced the performance of production establishments. This is no longer true and it is the availability of highly educated and highly skilled labour that is becoming an increasingly important issue for the IT production sector. As a result, the spatial distribution of the IT sector is being skewed towards core regions as these are best able to support the growth of the industry. Moreover, labour migration tends to be into core regions, further stregthening the ability of such areas to sustain the IT industry.

In summary, the full range of labour issues in the IT production sector is characterised by restructuring. Growth in output corresponds to, at best, jobless growth, but more commonly *job-loss* growth. Employment practices are being 'enhanced', with the focus placed upon the individual and their contribution to work. In consequence, attributes (that is, social skills) are becoming dominant employment selection criteria. Further, the notions of skill shortage may reflect the poverty of manpower, planning, archaic employment and a reluctance to invest in people rather than a consistent failure of labour markets to perform effectively.

INFORMATION AND TECHNOLOGY

Beyond the realm of IT production and its technologically orientated policies lies a complex of policy issues concerned with the commodification and trade in information. Within the context of a Schumpeterian analysis these issues are inextricably linked with those policies designed to support the carriers of the new technological paradigm. The major economic impact of IT products lies not in themselves but in their application to information. Increasingly, it is the realisation of new economic opportunities associated with the capture, storage, processing and communication of information that is central to economic growth. The purpose of this section is to consider, albeit briefly, some of the broader issues that arise as a result of this potential to trade in information. In so doing, however, the emphasis tends to move from diagnosis to prognosis.

IT products have most successfully penetrated sectors in which information *per se* has been the essential nature of the business. For example, the banking sector[15] has been able to assimilate the technology readily because it has been introduced primarily as a process substitution; the nature of the business has remained the same. Similarly, for applications such as accounting and word processing the technology has been applied to existing data manipulation problems. In contrast, the introduction of IT to manufacturing cannot proceed without a fundamental review of the nature of the business. The introduction of the technology requires *information* to be the explicit axiom upon which the business is organised. A computer-aided design (CAD) system is not cost-effective as a drawing board substitute, its efficacy is dependent upon its ability to organise and control information. The efficacy of a CAD system is fully realised only as part of a computer intergrated manufacturing (CIM) system. The technology, therefore, poses substantial organisational problems both within the firm and in its relationships with other firms.

The integration of IT objects into processes and products necessarily increases both the information content and communication capabilities of such products and processes. As a result, value added is being transferred explicitly to the information embedded in products and processes. Further, the changes brought about by the inclusion of information *technology* results in products and processes being drawn into systems rather than standing as discrete elements. The creation of systems both blurs the distinction between products and processes, and increases their potential transportability.[16] This blurring of products and processes also leads to the blurring of sectoral boundaries; for example, General Motors has emerged, as a result of its investments in IT, as a leading company in factory automation and is also the largest credit agency in the USA. The extent, however, to which transportability is achieved depends both on the development of communications infrastructure and the extent to which the information embedded with products and processes is traded as a commodity. As a result, communication networks are becoming 'marketplaces' and the nature of access to the network is shaping participation in an information dominated economy. The growth in the 'network marketplace' is best understood in the context of transborder data flows (TDF) for such an approach encompasses the totality of intercorporate and intracorporate communications, their international perspectives, and the division of these communication flows between private and public domains. The tension between private and public communications infrastructures, and the implications upon economic development in a information age, throws the telecommunications re-regulatory debate that is raging in most OECD nations into sharp focus.

The communications infrastructure
The axiom upon which communication infrastructures have been built and regulated throughout the world is, in essence, the exchange of monopoly operating rights (or heavily circumscribed competition) for the provision of services universally. Telecommunications service delivery has been recognised as a natural monopoly. There has, however, been a reversal of this policy in recent years in key OECD nations initiated by the divestiture of AT&T and the deregulation of key telecommunication markets in the USA. New regulatory regimes have been introduced which have encouraged the growth of competition in the UK; for example, Mercury Communications has been licensed as a national competitor to British Telecommunications PLC. The effect of these new regulatory regimes in the USA and the UK has led to spatial inequalities in services measured both by type, quantity and quality of service.[17] New entrants have invested in spatially concentrated markets, whilst at the same time attempting to satisfy the

total communications needs of major clients which, by definition, are spatially disparate.[18] The new entrants have based their competitive advantage upon a lowest cost strategy, whilst by contrast the established producers have based their competitive advantage on economies of scale and scope derived from their extensive telecommunications networks. In consequence, new entrants are forced to increase the scope of their telecommunications networks, whilst the incumbents are simultaneously investing in new facilities on high-density routes in order to reduce carriage costs, and rebalancing their tariffs in favour of large corporate users. As a result the telephone companies are being allowed to skew the incremental development of what is essentially a public infrastructure in order to maximise benefits to their private shareholders. This necessarily leads to a conflict of interest and, as observed by Borrous *et al.* (1984) a failure to capture full benefits for society as a whole: 'There is a real risk that the full gains of new telecommunications will never be captured by the US economy and polity so long as the private market alone — major users and providers — administer infrastructural change'.

In short, access to the (information) marketplace is being circumscribed by the differential development of the infrastructure both spatially and functionally. Thus, the opportunities for addressing such issues as regional disparities in employment income between households are lost, and the emerging information economy will exacerbate these problems, not alleviate them.

CONCLUSIONS

The main theoretical thrust that exists throughout this chapter is that a Schumpeterian view offers an understanding of IT that highlights implications of both the technology and the consequent capabilities and opportunities for the commodification of information. It is this focus of the framework upon innovation and its consequences that yields important insights into developments in IT.

In terms of the IT production sector, considerable attention has been given to the policy implications of the *technology* and the need to maintain a leading position in development of the technology. It is clear, however, that within the corporate sector, the risks of maintaining an involvement in leading edge technologies during a period of rapid change in technology and customer requirements are greater than any one company can sustain. In consequence, new groupings of companies are emerging through strategic alliances. However, these alliances, which are essentially based on the exchange of technology for market access, pose major problems for policy initiatives which are developed on a national, or even perhaps on a supranational scale (for example, European Community). These problems relate to the exacerbation of trade deficits, the potential loss of research and development and the development of barriers to entry created through the exchange of information.

In parallel to the development of strategic alliances, there has been the widespread adoption of JIT manufacturing systems. The benefits are far more profound than first stock externalisation and lie essentially in increased responsiveness to a volatile and internationally competitive environment. The costs, however, involve the reorganisation of the firm, a revaluation of activities and the shedding of those that cannot be provided competitively, and the adherence to fault-free quality standards.

The forces of technology are not only creating volatility in the marketplace, but also within the firm in terms of changing sources of value added, and this, in turn, is having an impact upon both the level of employment and the skill composition of the work-force. Advances in technology are permitting substantial increases in output with little, if any, increase in employment. Moreover, changing sources of value added are leading to a bifurcated work-force with, on the one hand, the decline in skilled and semi-skilled employment and, on the other, increasing employment of professional and scientifically qualified employees.

However, the degree of attention paid to the technological aspects of IT beguiles the need to recognise and grapple with the commodification of information. The growth of information markets, however fledgling, is an extension of the general integration of IT objects into products and processes.

In concert with the development of tradable information there is the need to create information marketplaces — a communications infrastructure. Increasingly, the incremental development of the communications infrastructure is being left to the private sector and is thus skewed towards existing major routes and clients, and possible restrictions on access. Governments are rejecting their historically held perception that infrastructure regulation is best built upon the notion of universality of service provision in exchange for restricted, if any, competition. Instead, they are adhering to the tenets of competition as the theoretical foundations of their regulatory policy. In consequence, there is a danger that the opportunities of new economic activity associated with IT will not be evenly distributed between nations, regions, businesses and households; at best existing inequalities will remain.

In short, there is a concern that the proliferation of IT technology policy initiatives witnessed since the late 1970s will turn out to be no more than placebos designed for specific symptoms. There is a need to understand the full implications of IT both in terms of the technology and its impact on the transformation of existing production processes, particularly upon the emergence of an information economy. Unless policy is developed upon such understanding its effectiveness will always be subject to question.

REFERENCES

1 For example, McKinsey and Co. (1983); Mackintosh (1986).
2 For example, issues of extra territoriality, temporal restrictions, total restrictions and partial availability were highlighted in a report by ACARD (1986) on the software industry. These issues are also central to the current (February 1987) debate on US Department of Commerce monitoring British firms and their use of imported American technology, including information.
3 The concept of a 'network marketplace' is described by Dordick *et al.* (1981) as follows: 'A network marketplace will result from the establishment of low cost computer-communication networks. These networks will provide the transport system for information products and services so that a mass production, mass distribution, mass marketing and mass consumption information processing industry can develop, much like other historic advances in transport.'
4 These arguments have been put by, for example, Freeman (1984).
5 See *Financial Times*, 12 February 1986.
6 Alternative names for JIT are *kan-ban* (Japanese), or continuous flow manufacturing.
7 For example, Mortimer (1986).
8 For example, Estall (1985).
9 See *Financial Times*, 12 February 1986.
10 See Sayer and Morgan (1984).
11 See Williams and Charles (1986).
12 See *Financial Times*, 2 February 1987.
13 See, for example, evidence to House of Lords Select Committee on Employment (1985).
14 See Williams *et al.* (1985).
15 See Rada (1984).
16 It has been estimated that the UK banking sector has some 15,000–20,000/man years invested in software ACARD 1986).
17 See Pike and Mosco (1985), also Taylor and Williams (forthcoming, 1987).
18 See Langdale (1983).

BIBLIOGRAPHY

ACARD (1986) *Software. A Vital Key to UK Competitiveness*, Cabinet Office, HMSO.
Borrus, M., Bar, F. and Warde, I. (1984), 'The impacts of divestiture and deregulation: infrastructural changes, manufacturing transition and competition in the US telecommunication industries', BRIE Working Paper, Berkeley, California.
Dordick, H., Nauss, B. and Bradley, H. (1981), *The Emerging Network Marketplace*, Beverley Hills, Sage.
Estall, R. C. (1985) 'Stock control in manufacturing, the Just-in-Time system and its locational implications', *Area, XVII* (2), June.
Freeman, C. (1984), *Long Waves in the World Economy*, Butterworths, London.
Gorbis, M. (1985), *From Conglomeration to Confederation: Organisational and Management Challenges in the 1980s*, SRI International.
House of Lords Select Committee on Employment (1985), HMSO.
Langdale (1983), Competition in the US long distance telecommunication industry, *Regional Studies*, June, pp. 393–409.
Mackintosh, I. (1986), *Sunrise Europe: the Dynamics of Information Technology*, Blackwells, Oxford.
McKinsey & Co. (1983), A Call for Action: the European Information Technology Industry, Report to Commission of the European Community, Brussels, January.
Mortimer (1986), *Just in Time: An Executive Briefing*, Institute of Fiscal Studies.
Pike, R. and Mosco, V. (1985), From luxury to necessity and back again? Canadian consumers and the pricing of telephone services in historial and comparative perspectives, *Working Paper No. 5, Studies in Communication and Information Technology*, Queens University, Kingston, Ontario.
Rada, V. F. (1984), Development Telecommunications and the Emerging Service Economy, Paper to Second World Conference on Transborder Data Flow Policies, Rome, June.
Sayer, A. and Morgan K. (1984), A modern industry in a declining region: link between method, theory and policy, in D. Massey and R. A. Meegan (eds), *The Politics of Method*, Methuen, London.
Taylor, J. and Williams, H. (1987), *Regulatory Change and Organisational Responses: Unintended Consequences in Telecommunications Policy Making*, CURDS, Newcastle University, Mimeo.
Williams, H. and Charles, D. (1986), 'The electronics industry in the North East: growth or decline?', *Northern Economic Review* (13), Summer.
Williams H., Thwaites, A. T., Gillespie, A. E. and Howells, J. (1985) 'The Location and Development of Information Technology Production with the Community', Report to Director-General, Regional Policy European Commission.

ACKNOWLEDGEMENT

The discussion of the IT production sector is drawn from a research project undertaken by the Centre for Urban and Regional Development Studies at the University of Newcastle Upon Tyne for the European Commission. This project would not have been possible without the full support and involvement of A. T. Thwaites, A. E. Gillespie, J. Howells, D. Charles and C. Pywell. Any errors, however, in interpretation or presentation remain the author's.

Government regulation and innovation in information technology

DAVID J. GOODMAN
AT & T (Bell)

INFORMATION TECHNOLOGY AND SOCIETY

Information age is a term used to describe an emerging era of social, economic and political activity in the developed world. Already, the combined influence of computers and communications has set in motion changes in society as profound as those of the Industrial Revolution that began 200 years ago. Political and economic power, which shifted from landowners to capitalists in the Industrial Revolution, is now moving to the people and organisations that control the storage and flow of information. (How many governments perform their first deeds at the national broadcasting station and their final ones at the paper shredder?) Paid employment in the information age will consist far more of manipulating information than producing and distributing food, raw materials and finished products. Education, health care, leisure activities and even the creative arts are increasingly centred on sounds and images that have been produced, recorded or transmitted electronically.

Anticipating the information age, we can be optimistic about reversing many of the abuses that we have come to identify with the Industrial Revolution. Information technology (IT) does not pollute the environment, it makes few demands on scarce natural resources, it consumes little energy and it asks little in the way of demanding human labour. On the other hand, it threatens to disrupt our accustomed pattern of life by eliminating more jobs than it creates, and it threatens personal liberty by providing powerful new techniques for surveillance and persuasion, and by making them easily accessible to centralised authority.

Societies that seek for their members both the benefits of the information age and the preservation of individual liberties are faced with the need to create a legislative and administrative framework for the new technology. The rate of technical advance today exceeds the stately pace of social and political evolution. As a consequence, we find ourselves with institutions and traditions that made sense when they originated, but which are now inconsistent with each other and with their original purposes. Conversely, we must also recognise that technological progress does not occur in a social vacuum; its nature, speed and direction are strongly influenced by the institutions and attitudes of the society in which it takes place.

History has many examples of technology stimulating profound social changes. An ancient example is the invention of printing which led to a vast expansion of literacy and drastically altered relationships between individuals and organisations. Efficient postal services and later telegraphy reinforced these effects but it was not until the invention and commercial development of the telephone 100 years ago that a new medium of telecommunications, voice transmission, was possible. While the telephone changed the nature of interpersonal communications, radio broadcasting created new possibilities for communication from large organisations to population masses. Photography, motion pictures and television added visual information to the repertory of communication media that already included text and sounds. Each of these inventions had an immediate impact on the communitites in which they were introduced. This catalogue of social changes stimulated by innovations is characteristic of historical developments and of the present-day impact of new information age technology.

Looking ahead to the next century, we can expect the process to be reversed. There is now coming into existence such a broad range of new capabilities that the specific products and services that emerge from them will be determined by social requirements and values. The means will exist to create an enormous diversity of information services and the successful innovators will be the ones who anticipate human desires rather than those who push back the frontiers of technology. Transportation has been on a similar technological plateau for the past quarter century. There are many possibilities, and changes in transportation are stimulated far more by social and political forces than by advances in technology.

INFORMATION TECHNOLOGY AND GOVERNMENT ACTIVITY

It is the purpose of this chapter to examine today's two-way interactions between government regulation and innovation in information technology. Of course it is impossible to explore this subject comprehensively here — the range of government activities influencing information technology is vast. For example, we have in the UK the common law traditions of free speech and a privileged press, traditions reflected in the USA in the First Amendment to the Constitution. Thus we see, at the foundations of our societies, strongly entrenched principles of government non-interference in printed and spoken communications. We can call this the *philosophical* end of the range of government interest in information. At the other extreme we find, in the management of the radio spectrum, the *technical* aspect of government activity. Here, in common with almost every other nation, the American and British governments play a very explicit role in controlling access to the airwaves and in determining the content of the communications that take place. Indeed, for a long time the British government reserved public broadcasting for itself and still, through the British Broadcasting Corporation (BBC), plays a major role in this area of IT.

In his book,[1] *Technologies of Freedom* (1983), Ithiel de Sola Pool, points to the merger in the information age of printed communications, which have been governed by the philosophical principle of freedom, and electronic communications, which have been governed by the technical principle of controlled access. The book explores the inevitable clash of these two principles and speculates on its effects on individual freedom. Several factors contribute to the blurring of the boundary between print and electronic media. Computerised word processing and the transmission of newspaper contents to dispersed printing plants inject a strong electronic component into text publishing. They also produce economies of sale that tip the competitive balance in the publishing industry in favour of powerful organisations with control over large segments of their markets. Amplifying this effect in the USA is the widespread ownership of broadcast companies by newspaper and magazine publishers.

Radio, however and, to a smaller extent, television broadcasting no longer have to be the exclusive domains of the rich and powerful. Low-power local broadcasting facilities and cheap cable television access can disperse control of broadcast media at the same time that other developments have concentrated control of print media. Combined, these factors undermine some of the original justifications for close regulation of electronic communications (limited access) and for press freedom (easy access).

Beyond promoting freedom of some types of communications and strictly regulating others, governments play many other roles in the progress of IT. The treatment of much information is covered by copyright; inventions are encouraged and protected by patent law; technology is retarded or stimulated by labour law; taxation, investment incentives; and the list goes on. Finally, I must at least mention the enormous effect on the future of IT in the USA of the antimonopoly principles that led to the fragmentation of AT & T. Correspondingly in the UK the government's treatment of British Telecom has had, and will continue to have, profound effects on the evolution of the information age.

The mirror image of these influences of government on IT is the influence of new technology on government activity. I have already pointed out that in the information age, the boundary between printed and electronic information is being effaced and may one day disappear. Governments will have to reconcile the divergent principles of regulation that have traditionally been applied to these converging modes of information. Copyright definitions and enforcement have to be redefined in an era of electronic copying machines and magnetic recording of sound and video. Patent law has been overtaken by the growing software content of information age inventions. And a major force behind the AT & T divestiture was the impossibility of separating computers and communications systems as mandated by existing regulations.

We are all capable of making long lists of government influence on the progress of IT and information age innovations that cry out for changes in laws and administrative procedures. To address the subject in more depth, I will, in the remainder of this chapter, focus on one aspect of IT, (telecommunications) and on one form of government activity (radio spectrum management). I will first present my view of the future of telecommunications. Then I will discuss traditional and evolving approaches to spectrum management. Finally, I will argue that these parallel trends in innovation and government activity are serving to reduce, rather than heighten the contradictions between traditional regulation and new technology.

TRENDS IN TELECOMMUNICATIONS

The wealth of communications possibilities in the twenty-first century will result from the convergence of several current research and development activities including: (a) the creation of integrated digital communications networks carrying all forms of information — textual, numeric, acoustic and pictorial; (b) the deployment within these networks of lightwave communications systems with the capacity to convey extremely large quantities of information efficiently; and (c) the development of intelligent, flexible interfaces that make it easy for human users to gain access to the network no matter where they are and to control it in a natural manner.

Integrated digital services

Two global communications networks, postal and telephonic, each made up of more than 100 linked national networks, serve the majority of the world's population. A key ingredient of the information age is the vision of a new communications network that combines the nearly instantaneous quality of telephony with diversity of services characteristic of postal communications. Just as post offices today all handle postcards, letters, parcels and printed materials, each item with its own priority (express, first class, etc.), there will in the future be an integrated telecommunications network using common facilities for voice communications, computer data, television, facsimile, alarms and control signals.

The key to the creation of a generalised telecommunications network is the recognition that all information can be represented in digital form. This is obvious in the case of computer data or even text which is inherently digital. However, it is also true of sounds and pictures and other types of information which are normally represented in analog formats; for example, as continuous fluctuations in light intensity, colour or sound pressure. The network of tomorrow, often referred to as ISDN,[2] (Integrated Services Digital Network), will evolve as a merger of resources and techniques currently in place in telephone systems and in hundreds of specialised networks such as those that provide computer communications, facsimile, cable television, electronic funds transfers and airline reservations.

Today's rapid progress towards a global ISDN reflects the desire of communications equipment manufacturers and operating authorities to market their products and services in an international arena. This has led them to put aside considerations of short-term, localised advantages, such as those that have left us with a diversity of incompatible broadcast television formats. Instead they seek international agreement on standards that are sufficiently flexible to accommodate future technology and yet precise enough to permit simple communication between users with equipment from many different sources. The communications industries of the world recognise that, unlike many products such as automobiles which have intrinsic utility to their owners, most communications devices are of value only if they are compatible with products adopted by a larger user population.

The Open Systems Interconnection[3] (OSI) is an example of an approach to standardisation that has found widespread acceptance by manufacturers and service providers. The OSI, proposed by the International Organisation for Standardisation, identifies a seven-layer architecture for communications compatibility. The specific interfaces range from physical connections (including plugs and voltage levels) at the bottom layer, to applications (for example, text editing or robot manipulation) at the top layer. Intermediate layers include network functions (such as addressing and error control) near the bottom, and computing conventions (such as logging-in and languages) near the top. At present there is widespread acceptance of the seven-layer architecture and of specific standards for some of the lower layers. Formal standards at higher levels of the hierarchy are under discussion.

Whilst the OSI represents the point of departure for computer networks entering an ISND, the starting point for telephony is a set of standards adopted by the International Consultative Committee on Telegraphy and Telephony (CCITT). In contrast to the world of computers, the word 'digital' in ISDN represents a restraint on progress in telephony. Although there is a large and rapidly growing body of digital switching and transmission equipment in place, nearly all of the world's telephones and their connections to the telephone network remain analog. Because end-to-end digital connection is a basic ingredient of ISDN, there is intense interest in the CCITT recommendations for digital subscriber loops and a growing consensus that these circuits will accommodate three logical communications channels: two 'B' channels, each operating at 64 kilobits per second; and one 'D' channel, operating at 16 kilobits per second.

Sixty-four kilobits per second is the ubiquitous rate for telephone speech. It is used in all digital switching equipment (both within public networks and on customer premises) and over the vast majority of digital transmission facilities. Recognising that signal processing technology now makes it possible to represent telephone speech accurately at rates lower than 64 kilobits per second, CCITT has recently adopted a standard technique, adaptive differential pulse code modulation, for speech transmission at 32 kilobits per second. With the acceptance of this standard there is likely to be widespread application of 32 kilobits per second speech by private users and telephone operating companies seeking to reduce the costs of speech storage and long-distance transmission.

While ISDN is a vision of rapid transmission of all types of information over a single network spanning the entire world, present capabilities consist of a collection of procedures for accomplishing specific communications tasks. There is, however, ample motivation on the part of users, service providers and manufacturers to make the vision into more of a reality. To do so, they do not require new breakthroughs in switching and transmission, but instead they must first understand clearly society's communications needs and desires, and then organise existing techniques to fulfil them. The basic steps towards integrating voice and computer communications have already been taken. On the horizon is the extension of agreed communication formats and network capabilities to visual communications services such as television, surveillance systems, facsimiles, etc., which create demands for larger information capacities than those of telephones and computers.

Lightwave communications
The key to transporting information at these high rates is optical fibre transmission, a technique that has matured in a remarkably short span of time.[4] Although there has been optical transmission of digital information since primitive times (by means of signal fires and smoke signals, for example), the first optical fibres were created less than twenty years ago. Early laboratory materials existed in minute quantities and had attenuations of tens of decibels per kilometre. Now, the attenuation of mass-produced glass fibres is a small fraction (about 0·25) of one decibel per kilometre. Advances in the quality and economy of lasers and photodetectors have kept pace with the progress in optical fibres to the point that there are now few obstacles to achieving point-to-point lightwave communications with almost any required capacity. For example, the transatlantic cable scheduled for operation in 1988 will contain six fibres each transmitting 296 megabits per second, which adds up to the equivalent of 40,000 simultaneous telephone conversations. Terrestrial systems at 565 megabits per second are already in production and plans are in place for introducing 1·7 gigabit systems with 50 kilometre repeater spacings.

Meanwhile, theoretical studies and laboratory experiments clearly indicate that these already vast capacities are only a fraction of what can be expected. An example of a recent achievement is 4 gigabit per second transmission over 117 kilometres of fibre. In the area of long-distance transmission, the capacity of future systems will be much more limited by society's demand for the communication of huge quantities of information than by the, ability of engineers to supply it.

This is not to say that all practical lightwave communication problems have been solved. Although it is rapidly becoming possible to transmit almost any desired amount of information from one place to another, the assembly of all that information from a diversity of sources and its distribution to many destinations remain bottlenecks. The ability to switch and modify information in an optical format will add substantially to the performance and economy of optical communications systems that today convert signals to an electronic mode for processing and then back to light for further transmission. Scientists are presently experimenting with materials and devices for switching and multiplexing photonic signals. More ambitious than the aim of using these new devices to replace costly and slower electronic components is the vision of optical computing to sustain the momentum of increasing computational power beyond the physical limits of speed and power dissipation inherent in electronic computation.

Another goal for photonic communication is the creation of optical fibre networks with multiple entries and exits for information terminals and computers. These networks require the means of efficiently coupling light into, and extracting it from, fibres at many closely spaced points in an office, campus or local telephone exchange environment. This capability will open up the possibility of replacing coaxial cable, the common transmission medium in high-speed networks, with optical fibre, with its inherently higher capacity and lower susceptibility to electromagnetic interference. Not only do we require devices that add and extract information incrementally along the length of a fibre, but also we must make it a simple matter to insert, remove and rearrange these connections to facilitate the frequent changes that take place in local networks. And finally, there is a need for communications protocols matched to the properties of fibre networks in order to provide efficient, equitable and reliable sharing of the network resources among the devices connected to it.

Natural human access
Professor Colin Cherry used to say that the only automatic telephone system was the now nearly extinct manual switchboard. Grandfather

would say, 'I would like to speak with my daughter Jane', and the telephone company (i.e. the operator) would do the rest. Because she was in touch with all of the houses in the village, she would know that Aunt Jane was visiting Cousin Fred and was willing to accept calls from relatives. The operator would, therefore, put the call through to Fred's telephone, rather than Jane's. By contrast, most telephony today requires grandfather to go through a disciplined procedure, dialling exactly the right multidigit number, to obtain a connection to the pair of wires entering Jane's house. If Jane is not at home, and grandfather is eager to speak to her, he can guess at her movements, obtain some likely telephone numbers and try to reach her.

Although we take this situation for granted, it will be drastically altered in the next few decades so that twenty-first century telephone users will interact with an electronic version of the village operator. Not only will this operator be able to reach Jane at Fred's house in the next street, but it will also be able to locate her in a different town, even a different country. Nor need she be at a fixed location. Perhaps the caller will find her in her car or walking about with a portable telephone.

In some places consumers can now obtain an assortment of products and services that perform some of the operator's functions. For example, there are repertory dialers that store Aunt Jane's phone number and dial it when grandfather pushes the right button or types in a short code. He can even buy a product that exploits state-of-the-art voices recognition technology to decide that he has said 'Jane' and then proceed to dial Jane's number for him. At the other end of the call, Jane may have a cordless phone so that she need not come in from the garden to answer the call. She may also have access to an automatic rerouting service provided by her local phone company or the private branch exchange in her office. With this service she can have her calls sent to Fred's phone when she goes to visit him. Or, more impressively, Jane may subscribe to a cellular radiotelephone system that will ring the phone in her car no matter where it is in a geographical area that may be as vast as the entire Scandinavian Peninsula. Like customer-controlled rerouting capabilities, cellular radio relies on switching machines controlled by flexible, reliable, realtime software. It derives bandwidth efficiency in densely populated areas from microprocessor control of lower-power mobile units which can change channel assignments as they move from one geographical cell to another, thus enabling the same frequencies to be used at many points simultaneously in a metropolitan area.

While these and many other new products and services of the 1980s provide components of the electronic village operator, they all possess severe limitations. The cordless phone will not work properly if too many neighbours buy them; if Jane leaves Fred's house to go to her hairdresser, she must first return home to have all calls redirected to her next stop; and it is fairly easy for eavesdroppers to listen to her cordless phone and cellular radio conversations.

To overcome these disadvantages and transform the present scattered collection of user adaptable, user friendly, mobile portable facilities into ubiquitous, intelligent, interface between humans and networks, we require a grand plan for harnessing the flexibility of modern switching machines, controlled by general purpose computers, to the wealth of vocal, visual and tactile channels of communications between machines and their human users. The devices that are not connected to the network by wires or optical fibres will have to share the open air electromagnetic spectrum, a limited resource with many competing claims for authorised access. In contrast to the abundant channel capacity of optical fibre communications, facilities that rely on open air transmission exist in an economy of bandwidth scarcity. Notwithstanding the impressive efficiency of cellular radio, digital open air communications will demand intensive application of efficient coding and modulation techniques. It remains to be seen to what extent and at what price the generous capacities allocated to terminals in the ISDN can be extended to non-wired services. To a large extent, the answer depends on social, economic and political priorities embodied in government allocation of radio channels.

TRENDS IN RADIO SPECTRUM MANAGEMENT

Spectrum management dates from the first quarter of the twentieth century when radio broadcasting came into existence on a large scale, The need for regulation seems apparent, The radio transmission medium is a scarce resource, the value of which is greatly diminished unless access is rationed and co-ordinated. Throughout the world governments have taken it upon themselves to do the rationing, However, the radio spectrum is only one of many scarce resources whose utilities depend on co-ordination. And, of course, solutions other than government rationing exist in the other domains. For example, in the USA's deregulated air transport industry, the competing airlines, rather than government regulators, co-ordinate takeoff and landing times in order to reduce congestion at airports. They do so to undo some of the effects of their first non-governmental approach to resource allocation — anarchy. We all experience this method of rationing a scarce resource whenever we travel by road.

Back to rationing and spectrum management. There are several stages in the rationing process. First, spectral band are allocated to specific services; then, there is a decision about the means of providing the service. Somewhere along the way there are decisions about the content of the service. Finally comes the licensing process — deciding who is to provide the service. The first two stages are relevant to the present topic: allocating frequencies to services, and defining the communications formats of the services. Both of these processes are strongly influenced by advances of technology. Sometimes the new technology opens up a new type of communication, such as Teletext. In other cases, it creates a better or more efficient way of providing an existing service. In either case, for society to have the benefit of the new technology, regulators must grant it access to the already crowded electromagnetic spectrum.

Conversely, just as technology places demands on regulators, the process of regulation influences the course of technology. The flow of new products and services depends on the perceived responsiveness or inertia of the regulatory process. Over the last decade, there has been mounting criticism of spectrum management in the USA on the ground that it strongly inhibits the invention and exploitation of new or improved means of communication.

How do regulators decide among conflicting demands for the same frequency bands? In the USA the main regulatory body, the Federal Communications Commission (FCC), is governed by the *Communications Act*, enacted in 1934, and amended piecemeal on several occasions since. Among the stated goals of the Act are to make available to all of the people of the USA an efficient, economical communication service that takes into account the requirements of national defence and safety of life and property. The FCC is directed to distribute 'licenses, frequencies, hours of operation and power among the several States and communities so as to provide a fair, efficient and equitable distribution of radio services'. It is further directed to 'encourage the introduction of new and additional services by new applicants, existing licensees and others'. However, the same paragraph of the Act that directs the encouragement of new services also states that the new services must not cause 'significant technical degradation to, or interference with, radio transmissions by other licensees'.

Thus we have a qualified mandate to stimulate new technology, and to many observers, the FCC, over the years, has leaned too much towards caution and away from stimulation. A strong message to this effect was provided by the United States Congress in 1982, when it added Section 7 to the *Communications Act*. This amendment shifts the burden of proof from proposers to opponents of new technologies and services. The opponents now have 'the burden to demonstrate that such proposal is inconsistent with the public interest'. Moreover, the FCC must, within one year, 'determine whether any new technology or service proposed ... is in the public interest'.

While all these goals and directions have apparent merit, they are only general guides to decision-making. In going about its business, the FCC has created an elaborate collection of rules and procedures for parcelling out and using the radio spectrum. In terms of responding to or influencing innovations, the most significant aspects of spectrum management by the FCC are found in four technical principles that guide many of the commission's procedures: efficiency, non-interference, quality and interoperability.

While these are technical aims with merits that transcend national boundaries, regulators are also guided by criteria that reflect the values of their own society. One criterion that was for a long time approached from opposite points of view in the UK and the USA is localism. For many years, broadcasting in the UK was a State monopoly; and, with the exception of very brief intervals of each day, it consisted of national coverage provided by a few stations.

At the same time, reflecting the federalism at the core of American political philosophy, the American government acted vigorously to ensure extremely localised access to the airwaves. With respect to radio and VHF television, the country is divided into 218 broadcast service areas and there are strict limits on ownership of facilities in more than one area. For example, the three powerful television networks in the USA own only five television stations each. In the case of UHF television and cable television, service is provided on a far more localised basis. This has led to the existence of 8000 radio stations, close to 1000 television stations and 4000 cable television systems.[5]

Five other examples of non-technical goals that play a role in spectrum management are (a) support for domestic economic interests in the face of foreign competition; (b) protection of the investments of existing licensees; (c) maintenance of a competitive market of services; (d) access to the airwaves for special groups, such as those served by religious, cultural and educational programming; and (e) the one embodied in Section 7 of the *Communications Act*, the rapid introduction of new services.

Outlook

The word 'deregulation' has been used with increasing frequency over the past decade to describe the direction of public attitudes to the control of many areas of economic activity in the UK and in the USA. The aim of the deregulators is to have industry shaped by competitive market forces rather than by explicit directives of governments and cartels. The pressure for deregulation has come from both ends of the political spectrum. On one side, it is seen as a movement that strenghens consumers against powerful commercial and industrial forces. On the other, deregulation is seen as an important step in removing restraints on economic progress imposed by centralised bureaucracy. Perhaps the strongest effects of deregulation have been felt in transportation and banking. However, the spirit of deregulation is pervasive. It has changed the substance of government regulation of cable television and telephony. It has already changed the style of radio spectrum management and a fundamentally new approach to controlling the airwaves waits in the wings.

Whilst traditional regulation, in principle, considers users of the radio spectrum to be trustees of public property, the new view is that a transmitting licence is a form of private property with intrinsic economic value to the licensee. The implication of this view is that the licensee should be able to use this property to his or her best advantage or to sell it or rent it at a price that reflects its value. Of course, freedom to use a frequency band to one's best advantage cannot be absolute. Just as in other forms of economic control (such as land ownership) restraints are necessary, primarily to prevent harm to neighbours. In this case the neighbours are operators in other frequency bands or in the same band in other geographical areas.

This invokes the principle of non-interference, one of the four technical criteria I mentioned as being at the heart of traditional radio spectrum management. The other ones are efficiency, quality and interoperability. In today's mood of deregulation, it is only the need for interference control that goes unchallenged. And even here there is a trend toward establishing a general framework, consisting of restrictions on emission levels, as opposed to a precise definition of all the details of the transmission.

Like non-interference, efficient use of the radio spectrum is generally acknowledged to be essential. By contrast, however, it is vigorously argued that this goal can be better realised in a deregulated environment. Traditionally, frequency bands are allocated to specific services with transmissions conforming to precise specifications. Until the specifications are established, there are strong incentives for competing manufacturers and service providers to achieve high efficiency. After the transmission formats are specified and licences are issued, however, there are few incentives to improve efficiency. Regulators tend to be highly respectful of the investments of licensees in equipment that conforms to the original specifications. Technology becomes fossilised and innovation dries up. The cycle can only begin anew when regulators hold out the hope of introducing new services to previously unavailable frequency bands.

This situation creates a regulatory dilemma. As soon as the nature of a service is specified precisely, there is little hope of improving its efficiency. Therefore, it is necessary to decide whether to introduce a new service at an early date, or to await technological enhancements that will give the public the advantages of improved efficiency. If so, the public is denied the benefits of the service during the waiting period.

This dilemma applies equally to quality. In the case of both quality and efficiency, deregulators argue that these goals can best be served when licence holders are given substantial freedom to use their frequency bands to their best advantage. Provided there is competition, this situation should create strong incentives to create new means of communications with better combinations of efficiency, quality and cost.

While considerations of interference, efficiency and quality are important in most economic spheres, interoperability plays a special role in innovation in IT. It means that the value of a product or service is not intrinsic, as, for example, in the case of an car but instead it depends on other people owning compatible products or subscribing to the same service. This is obvious in the case of telephony. As more and more people obtain telephone service, the value of the service to everyone increases because each subscriber has the possibility of speaking to an increasing number of people. This is true provided that all telephones are compatible. Interoperability is also important in other information services. The value of many computer products depends on the range of software applications they support as much as on their inherent characteristics, such as memory and speed.

This phenomenon affects innovation in IT. It means that a new product or service has not only to be better than its existing counterpart, but that its precise form has to be widely accepted in order for it to be of any value at all. One way to insure this acceptance is to have it prescribed by government. Until recently we have taken this area of regulation for granted in the case of services and products involving radio transmissions. When the PAL standard of colour television was adopted in the UK, broadcasters all transmitted in the PAL format and consumers confidently bought PAL receivers. On the other hand, an entirely different situation has occurred in the case of magnetic recording. In audio, alongside the cassettes that are today ubiquitous, there were eight-track tapes; and in video, the shops still have both VHS and Beta machines and tapes for sale. This fragmentation inhibits rapid dissemination of new information services. Conversely, one reason for the great success of audio compact discs is the fact that there is only one recording format in use and all machines can play all discs.

This came about through industry agreement rather than government decisions. And likewise, deregulators argue that many services involving radio transmissions do not necessarily require standardisation by government decree. They can converge as a result of agreements among private organisations or they can remain fragmented. This is not for governments to decide except in certain cases, such as services that provide for public safety.

In recent years, the FCC has decided to regulate interoperability much less vigorously than in the past. It is interesting to observe the contrasting effects on two new services, stereophonic television sound broadcasting and stereophonic AM (medium wave) radio. In both cases the FCC permits broadcasters to transmit stereo signals in any format they choose within certain constraints. In the case of television sound, the FCC perceived a high degree of similarity among the various proposals and pointed to one technique as nominally acceptable, though not required. (FCC officials refer to this form of approval as 'sprinkling holy water'). Today, in the USA, it is possible to buy stereophonic television recievers and there are many stereo broadcasts each day.

By contrast, the commission saw less agreement among the stereophonic AM proposals and chose not be bless any of them. And, as yet, there are no AM stereo broadcasts or equipment. Industry is reluctant to make investments in this risky environment. A succinct response to concern about this brake on the introduction of AM stereo is to be found in the comments of Commissioner Tyrone Brown: '... the interested parties want this agency to assist them in marketing this marginal service by aggregating the market into a single system. I see no reason in policy why we should accommodate this desire'.[6] The FCC's decision on AM stereophonic broadcasting reflects its current attitude towards regulation: The commission elects 'to permit broadcasters to employ any non-interfering transmission system and to allow the marketplace to determine which system or systems shall become dominant. [This] will encourage maximum technological innovativeness and competition and will avoid the increased costs to the public generally associated with the grant of monopoly rights.[7]'

Thus, the trend is strongly in the direction of less regulation with a growing body of opinion that favours treating the radio spectrum as a form of private property with economic value to its holder. In the USA, proponents of this point of view urge ownership of the spectrum. A recent article by Dr David Rudd, of the British government,[8] proposes a renting system. Contrasted with a growing consensus that ownership or rental is the correct approach to spectrum management in the long run, is uncertainty about how to introduce them initially. Whether or not governments go as far as treating transmitting licences as valuable, marketable property, it seems clear that regulatory trends will continue in the direction of permissiveness within bounds. The aim will be to service the public good through competition and market forces rather than by government directives.

CONSISTENCY OF TRENDS

A central theme of this paper is that armed with an abundance of technological alternatives, the users of IT, rather than the inventors and developers, will determine the nature of the emerging information age. This social influence will be felt in two ways: through the ephemeral 'invisible hand' of market forces and through tangible government action. In both the UK and the USA in recent years, governments have sought to shift the balance of control toward the marketplace and away from their own agencies. Both countries have made substantial changes in the economic structures of their national telephone networks. The aim is to diversify control because it is felt that in a competitive, rather than monopolistic environment, consumers will best be able to express their preferences for products and services and speedily gain access to the benefits of new technology.Concurrent with the stimulation of competition is deregulation of the content of communications services and of the technical means of providing the services.

In my view, a deregulated, competitive marketplace and an abundance of technological choices work consistently to produce products and services consistent with the public will. Deregulation brings to electronic information the principle of free expression that has, in the

USA and the UK, traditionally been applied to speech and printed material. As in other aspects of modern capitalist society, safeguards are necessary to prevent abuse of the weak by the powerful. In the technical arena, governments will continue to protect the rights of service providers by enforcing principles of non-interference. As the break-up of AT&T indicates, they will act to prevent undue accumulations of economic power by taking measures to promote competition. Through laws such as the *Freedom of Information Act* in the USA and the *Data Protection Act* in the UK., they aim to preserve privacy and inhibit the use of information to acquire undue political power.

The best way of achieving these and other social goals, and the prospects of success, are the subjects of other papers in this Colloquium.

REFERENCES

1 De Sola Pool, I. (1983), *Technologies of Freedom*, Harvard University Press.
2 Irmer, T. (1986), 'An idea turns into a reality — CCITT activites on the way to ISDN', *Institute of Electrical and Electronic Engineers Journal on Selected Areas in Communications, SAC-IV* (3), May, pp. 316-19.
3 Jenkins, P. A., and Knightson K. G., (1984), 'Open systems interconnection — the reference model', *British Telecom Technology Journal, II* (4), September, pp. 18–25.
4 Li, T. (1985), 'Lightwave telecommunication', *Physics Today*, May, pp. 24–31.
5 Walters, I. (1982), 'Freedom for communications', in Poole, R. W., Jr (ed.), *Instead of Regulation*, Lexington Books, pp. 93–133.
6 United States Federal Communications Commission (1980), 'Commissioner Brown issues dissenting statement on FCC's instructions to staff to propose selection of Magnavox's AM stereo system', press release, 14 April. The commission later reversed its position and issued a final order consistent with Commissioner Brown's views.
7 United States Federal Communications Commission (1982), 'In the matter of AM stereophonic broadcasting', Docket no. 21313, report and order, 4 March.
8 Rudd, D. 'A renting system for radio spectrum?', *Institution of Electrical Engineers Proceedings, 133*, part A, 1 January, pp. 58–64.

British industrial policy and the information technology sector

JILL HILLS
City University, London

INTRODUCTION

Capitalist economies are predicated on the assumption that private companies will continuously search for comparative advantage against their competitors. Their aim is to make the best possible use of available resources, be they land, raw materials, labour, technology or capital. And in a capitalist world economy, increasingly governments are held to be responsible for their domestic economies, the same can be said of governments.

Within the post-war world economy certain industries have come to be seen as flagships of national pride, whilst certain technologies are seen by governments as crucial to the maintenance of comparative advantage on a national basis. Information technology (IT) began as the computer flagship, and has become the enabling technology for gains in productivity in a wide span of industrial sectors. Those countries whose IT industries have done best in the post-war world economy are the USA and Japan. Each has had the comparative advantage of large home markets, a well-educated labour force able to utilise and improve technology, and available capital for investment supplemented by support from government to industry. The mechanisms by which this support has been delivered have differed considerably. In the USA they have varied from defence-related research and development and procurement and the *Buy American Act*, to tariff and quota impositions and actual subsidisation of exports. In Japan, which now ranks second to the USA in its production of electronic goods, physical tariff barriers and direct government support have recently been less important than a highly skilled work-force, cheap capital, an undervalued yen and frenetic competition between companies co-ordinated by government. Non-tariff barriers have also played their part in retaining the largest proportion of the domestic market for Japanese companies.

In general, as tariff barriers on manufactured goods have become progressively reduced under the provisions of the General agreement on Tariffs and Trade (GATT) so non-tariff barriers have sprung up, each aimed at either protecting the existing domestic market against invaders, or giving some comparative advantage to domestic industry. Without such developments in a liberalised world economy comparative advantage would go to the companies with the largest home markets — in present conditions, the Americans and Japanese — and one would expect the dominance of companies in the global market to be replicated within any one domestic market, (Loxley, 1980). Hence, industrial policy practised by West — European governments is a strategy for the survival of their control over domestic economies, a control which is being continuously eroded by the liberalisation of the world economy and the more effective support of industry by competitive governments.

In this world scenario, IT has come to be seen as the saviour of Western European nations against the predations made into traditional industries by the cheap labour of Third World countires, and as the means by which national economies can be pulled out of recession. Hopes have been pinned on the comparative advantage to be gained by the introduction of microelectroncs into products and processes within manufacturing industry. This chapter provides a brief overview of the main aspects of British industrial policy towards IT and the problems with that policy. It attempts to explain how it is that the UK in 1985 came to have a £2·3 billion (US) balance of trade deficit in the IT sector and suggests a future strategy to help reverse the current decline.

GOVERNMENT DEFINITION OF THE IT SECTOR

Definitions are obviously important because on them depend the goals of policy. The problem is that IT definitions used by government do not keep up with the changing boundaries of the industry, or the fluidity of the technology.

The ACARD report of 1980 included in IT:

important sectors of the electronic components industry (with an emphasis on microelectronics), much electronic equipment (notably computers and their associated terminals, displays etc) and the whole communications industry, including the broadcasting authorities and the Post Office. We further include the users and suppliers of information industrial, financial, commercial, administrative, professional and individual — because their activities will be affected by new forms of information handling. [para 1·7]

ACARD recommended the appointment of a Minister responsible for

co-ordination of government policies and actions on the promotion and development of IT and its applications through awareness, education and training, sponsorship of industry, provision of risk capital, public purchasing, publicly funded R&D, national and international regulations and standards, legislation, communications, and related programmes such as satellite technology [para 9·5]

In taking such a wide definition of IT and the measures which would be needed to promote the sector, the ACARD Committee was ahead of its time.

In practice the working definition of IT used in government has been heavily influenced by the administrative origins of the first sector programme, and the emphasis under the 1974–79 Callaghan Government on microprocessors. At that time the IT section of the Department of Trade and Industry was responsible for the sponsorship of computers and telecommunications manufacture and the Microelectronics Industry Support Programme (MISP), primarily aimed at attracting multinational investment in the manufacture of standard microchips. When the Minister for Information Technology was appointed in 1981, he became responsible primarily for this section and for the Microelectronics Applications Programme (MAP).

Even recent statements by government spokespersons do not retain the same definition. For instance, a Minister (*Hansard*, 21 January 1985, col. 278) defined IT as including office machinery, data processing equipment, telecommunications equipment, electrical instruments and control systems, radio and electronic capital goods, electronic components (including microelectronics and semi-conductors) and consumer electronics, but excluding tapes, records, software and computer services. Two months later (*Hansard*, 19 March 1985 col. 444) in a written reply he stated that the activity headings which were 'regarded as constituting the information technology industry' excluded electrical instruments and control systems. This government definition excludes all software and broadcasting and some hardware.

The NEDC uses a more restricted definition of the IT sector:

> the industry created by the convergence of computers and telecommunications and which comprises the manufacturing and supply of those products plus office systems and computer services. [NEDC, 1982, p. 1]

This definition is predominantly hardware oriented.

When no official bodies, not even the Department of Trade and Industry, can define an industrial sector in the same way twice, there is obviously room for a great deal of ambiguity and misunderstanding in policy. And when the definitions do not themselves match what is happening in the global industry then the effect on strategy is likely to be detrimental. The problem is not new — for many years the computing, telecommunications and microelectronics industries were treated as separate industrial sectors in British government policy, even as it became evident that vertical and horizontal integration was taking place within industry.

Whereas even four years ago it was possible to talk as if computing and telecommunications hardware were the primary components of an IT sector, today transmission is at the core of the sector. Transmission provides the link between the equipment manufactures, customers and information providers, be those providers of traditional software such as films or TV programmes, or interactive software, such as the new financial information services, equipment marketing, transmission and information provisions are all becoming interdependent. Specialised information services and transmission provide the consumer link, both national and international, for the marketing of equipment. In this context, to exclude transmission from a definition of the IT sector seems anachronistic. Similarly, it seems anachronistic to make the distinction between telecommunications and data processing manufacture or between software and hardware production, when software is now the predominant cost in any hardware product.

Yet these divisions are not simply statistical tools, but are replicated within government administration. In 1982 the NEDC (pp. 55–8) estimated that there were at least twenty-nine executive bodies in government with responsibility for IT, before OFTEL and the Cable Authority were created to oversee telecommunications transmission and cable TV, respectively, and before the IBA was made responsible for the regulation of Direct Broadcasting by Satellite (DBS). Today within the Department of Trade and Industry the five policy divisions directly concerned with the IT sector, as defined by the 1980 ACARD Committee, have offices in three separate buildings. Telecommunications transmission and sponsorship is separated from that for value added networks, from that for the computer industry, and from that for software, both in terms of administrative divisions and in physical location.

TECHNOLOGICAL CONVERGENCE AND AMERICAN DEREGULATION OF TELECOMMUNICATIONS

One of the major problems facing the industry and government policy in the IT sector is the dominance of American companies. Since the 1960s IBM has been dominant worldwide in data processing. It now supplies about 70 percent of the user base in Western Europe and, if IBM-compatible machines are also assumed to be under its indirect control, has a virtual monopoly of operating software. Until the 1980s the UK was the only country in which it did not take 50 percent of the domestic market, but the European Economic Community (EEC) directive which came into force in 1981 precluded preferential purchasing for large public sector data processing hardware contracts and, since that time, IBM has been taking a larger share of these. IBM's diversification and its more aggresive policy since its release from anti-trust constraints in the USA and Europe, has forced smaller companies to meet it head-on in mini and microcomputing with dire effects. In 1984 IBM toppled the British company ACT as market leader in the professional business computer market in the UK. Following its financial difficulties, BT has prevailed upon the British company to become a manufacturer of IBM-compatible machines, thereby illustrating the general problem facing computer companies.

The second major problem is that the companies involved in the sector are small by American or Japanese standards and have been losing world market share. This problem of size is important in an industry where lower unit costs emanate from mass production and global marketing. Software development costs have also been burgeoning and the blurring of distinctions between products and industries calls for new skills and products.

Already by the early 1980s the largest companies had assured themselves control over software design by vertical integration into component manufacture. Subsequently companies in one or other of the traditional computing or telecommunications industries have needed expertise and often marketing capability in additional products. Covergence has resulted in capital concentration and in numbers of technological and marketing agreements, often cross-national with a strong American or Japanese component, thereby increasing the penetration of products from those countries in Europe. The convergence of technologies has coincided with the break-up of AT & T in the USA and its release on to the world market. It has, therefore, been looking for and has found partners in Europe and its fight with IBM has been transferred into Europe. That fight has been translated into a battle of standards between Open Systems Interconnection (OSI) the one hand, backed by the European and Japanese manufacturers and AT & T and the System Network Architecture (SNA) standard of IBM on the other. OSI which will allow the interconnection of any make of computer, is intended to preclude the total domination by IBM of data transmission networks which would lock users into that company's computers.

Finally, as mentioned previously, there has been a movement of vertical integration between transmission and equipment manufacture and horizontal integration between information provision and transmission. For instance, IBM's takeover of Rolm, the telecommunications equipment manufacturer, has been followed by its buy out of other members of the Satellite Business Systems (SBS) transmission consortium and its subsequent sale of SBS to MCI, AT & T's major long-lines competitor. IBM has also linked with Merryl Lynch for the provision of information. In the UK BT has moved into telecommunications manufacture with its takeover of Canadian Mital, and is moving into information provision. And computer manufacturer, ICL, is moving into global network transmission. In Japan, equipment manufacturers have linked up with American transmission companies to provide Value Added Networks. In Japan, IBM is also co-operating with Nippon Telephone & Telegraph Corporation (NTT) to produce and market a small IBM computer — a move which may harm the European OSI strategy (Hills, 1986).

BRITISH POLICY

Government policy in the IT sector in the UK began in the 1960s with the Labour government's creation of the Industrial Reorganisation Corporation and the Ministry of Technology. In general, policies since that time which have involved public funding have been directed at mainframe data processing, defence electronics, telecommunications, and microelectronics (including microprocessors, computer-aided design and applications to products and processes). Areas of the industry in which there has been little overt government funding include the film industry, software (including data bases), peripherals, electronic 'brown' goods (such as TVs, radios, VCRs), and office equipment (such as copiers and typewriters).

In particular since 1979, the emphasis of government policy has been on technological push rather than market pull, on the sale of publicly financed companies such as Inmos, ICL and BT and on private sector financing of new ventures such as cable TV and DBS. In general, under both political parties, electronics research and development has been predominantly defence-oriented, with heavy emphasis on research rather than development, and multinationals have been welcomed with public money for their employment-enhancing prospects. Although there was, until 1981, a public sector purchasing policy in favour of ICL, this was never followed through into the whole public sector, and there has never been a policy of public procurement from British manufacturers. Market pull has been virtually ignored whilst, in recent years, both infrastructural investment and technology push investment have been reduced. Most importantly, the liberalisation of the telecommunications transmission market has increased imports in that area and reduced the scope of the public sector. In other cases decisions on national standards, such as cellular radio, have been taken which have increased imports immediately. These policies and those designed to increase the use of microelectronics in industrial products have been defended as improving competitiveness and increasing employment. Despite the lack of control over technology imported from the USA, which the *American Export Control Act* has underlined, the argument has been presented on the grounds that the origin of technology and products is irreleveant — only their use is important. Hence the user — manufacturer relationship and the protential development of user-based products for export have been ignored, whilst the manufacturing industry cannot rely on the fragmented domestic market for its volume sales.

INFRASTRUCTURAL STRATEGY

A strategy to effect a change to an economy based upon electronics from that based on old industries has to comprise certain key elements. Advanced technological processes can only be diffused, utilised and improved if the infrastructure of education, capital, and technology are in existence, if demand and supply are both fostered and if there is consensus that the technology benefits the nation — if it holds legitimacy. In the UK, despite almost twenty years of government policy towards parts of the IT sector, there is little evidence that either the infrastructure is in place or that the competitiveness of the industry on the world market is improving, rather the opposite. And, although trades unions have co-operated with the introduction of the new technology, there are already indications that IT is regarded as an elitist technology which will further divide those with access to it from those without.

A trained labour force
All estimates by industry and government since 1980 have shown a shortfall of trained personnel at all levels of the IT industry (Finniston, 1980, DTI, 1983, 1984, 1985; Northcott, 1986). Estimates of the size of that gap vary. In 1982 the Electronics NEDC estimated there had been a shortfall of 16,000 programmers/analysts and 7,000 engineers in 1980 (p. 24). The government working party set up to monitor the subject in 1985 estimated that demand for graduates in key areas would rise sharply — increasing by 24 percent for electrical engineering, 44 percent for maths, 61 percent for computer science and 21 percent for physics by 1990. But a 1984 study showed that the supply of electrical/electronic engineering and computer science graduates would actually fall annually between 1984 and 1986 by 10 percent-11 percent (*Guardian*, 22 January 1985). The working party estimated a shortfall of 1,500 in 1985, rising to 5,000 in 1987–88, but looked only at manufacturing industry and not users. The shortfall is replicated at lower levels, with estimates of a shortage of between 7,000 and 10,000 technologists and 30,000 technicians by 1988 (Manpower Services Commission (MSC) quoted in *Computer Weekly*, 5 April 1984). The majority of those entering the industry are men, women being an underused resource— only 5 percent of those graduating in IT are women — but policies to recruit girls into technological careers conflict with other current government ideology on the proper role of women.

A major problem in the area is that employers are unwilling to invest in training on the grounds that it costs about £7,000 to recruit and train a graduate, money which might not be recovered before the trainee moved on. They prefer, therefore, to take people with about two years experience. The government has argued that industry must do more of its own training, and by the withdrawal of public funding from some courses is attempting to force the issue. Industry has not taken up the challenge.

There have been short-term crisis responses, for instance, to 'convert' students from other disciplines to become IT specialists. Other responses at technician level (ITEC centres), set up initially with three-year funding, have now had that funding withdrawn and must become self-financing. An adult version of ITEC at nine of the MSC's skillcentres was introduced in 1984, but the skillcentres are also subject to threats of closure or privatisation. At one stage proposals were made by the national Computing Centre to train 350,000 young people in IT skills for specific industries such as banking, retailing or manufacture, but the scheme was turned down, it is said, when it was realised that greater numbers of youngsters could be accommodated in lesser skilled work, thereby bringing the unemployed numbers down. (*Computer Weekly*, 9 February 1984).

The government's Skill Shortages Committee which issued its last report in 1985 included representatives of government, education and the IT sector. Its major achievement was to get an extra £43 million allocation for additional engineering and technology places in higher education, and to set up another agency (IT Skills Agency) to liaise between industry and higher education. The government has also increased the numbers of posts and courses in IT available at university level (a swing of 0·5 percent to 1 percent taking place each year towards science and technology courses in universities). However, the overall number of undergraduate places at university reduced from peak of 84,695 in 1980 to 77,431 in 1984, so that any swings to science and technology are within a reduced overall total. The government also funded 250 'new blood' posts in universities, with particular emphasis on engineering and sciences. But the cuts in university finance in the early 1980s produced a greater level of voluntary redundancy among science and engineering staff, and cuts in university funding hit the technological universities most badly. The new posts do not necessarily make up the shortfall and there has also been difficulty in recruitment in competition with industry on the one hand and better working conditions in the USA on the other. The Electronics NEDC (1982, pp. 21–2) has also pointed to the 'creaming off' of British engineering talent by multinationals established in the UK whilst students have pointed out that employment in British electronics companies tends to involve employment in the defence sector.

The problem is actually more acute than the shortfall of engineers would suggest, since the numbers of graduates entering teaching in the science subjects is diminishing, leading to a knock-on effect in both the numbers of young people qualified to enter engineering courses and the quality of maths and science instruction available to all school children. Cuts in resources devoted to education and the holding down of public sector salaries have helped to undermine science courses in schools where, for instance, test tubes and other equipment may not be replaced, or insurance for computing equipment cannot be afforded. Hence, government policies of cutting public expenditure help to undermine its vision of a high technology UK (Prais and Wagner quoted in *Financial Times*, 23 May 1985).

Programmes intended to diffuse computing knowledge into schools have been hardware based, with only £2·5 million made available for software development. Teacher training has had to be done in teachers' own time and at their own expense, local authorities often now being unwilling to second teachers to year-long courses because of manpower and financial implications, Nor it is clear that the computing courses in schools are not merely replication the divisions between the 'haves' and the 'have-nots', — a lack of hands-on practice within schools due to shortage of machines demanding private ownership of equipment. Lack of machines and software make it unrealistic to think of hands-on experience for more than a minority, or of a breakdown in the sex-stereotyping of IT skills which occurs in children in their early teens.

The response of the Department of Education and Science (DES, 1985) to those concerned with standards of educational attainment has been to criticise employers for demanding that staff to be employed with new technology should be qualified in mathematics, and to try to establish both new vocationally based qualifications within secondary schools and a wider 'A' lever syllabus. But as schools increasingly rely on parents for the provision of essential items of equipment, the gap widens between rich and poor schools, and access to the new technology becomes a luxury.

The provision of capital
In a survey published in 1986 the most common difficulty companies found in the introduction of microelectronics into products was the shortage of staff (Northcott, 1986, p. 63). The next most common difficulties were the high cost of development, and lack of money to finance development, 30 percent of respondents mentioning each as a major difficulty. Software problems seem to take longer to iron out and are more expensive than companies expect. Even large firms have problems funding the required research and development. The City

looks to short-term profits rather than capital growth, penalising those companies who spend large amounts of money on future products. Hence, the possibility that Plessey might invest in a new public exchange switch has raised comments from the City that the institutional shareholders would not want to hold its stock. (*Sunday Times*, 3 August 1986). The situation in the UK is considerably different in this respect from that in either the USA or Japan, and companies argue that they should be given tax relief on research and development, as in both Japan and West Germany, to help combat the problem.

Public funded support for innovation
In 1983 the UK spent £7·33 billion on research and development — 2·3 percent of GDP — and a decrease of 2 percent on the 1981 proportion. The figure compares with 2·7 percent of GDP in the USA, 2·6 percent in West Germany and 2·5 percent in Japan, all of which increased their expenditure. In real terms, however, because the UK's GNP is declining and because of the increasing amount spent on defence, the total amount spent on civil research and development has been declining, so that the UK now devotes the lowest share of GDP to civilian research and development out of the five leading industrial nations. More than 50 percent of the UK's research and development expenditure is from government and more than 50 percent of that is devoted to defence. Half the total research and development on aerospace and electronics comes from the defence budget. Only 17 percent of total expenditure goes on civil industrial innovation, and private sector funding of research and development has been falling (European Commission, 1980; TUC, 1985; DTI, 1985).

Criticism of British defence-oriented research and development policy was first voiced in the 1970s by the government's then chief scientist Ieuan Maddock, but the trend towards defence research and development has continued. Almost ten years later (1983) he was able to demonstrate that there was not only little technological transfer between companies, but almost none within companies engaged in civilian and defence research and development. This lack of spin-off from defence into civil applications, which must partly be related to the secrecy involved, has led to doubts about the wisdom of taking part in the American SDI research programme, from both an industrial perspective and its usage of scarce personnel. Similar doubts about the SDI programme's impact on the supply of qualified labour for American industry and the spin-offs that might accrue to civilian technology have been raised in the USA (Council for Economic Priorities, 1985). By 1987 the programme is likely to consume 14 percent of the growth in American research and development and one in twenty-five of the 177,000 additional engineers to be employed between 1984 and 1987.

The British government is, however, in favour of British participation in the SDI programme. In contrast, it has been only after considerable hesitation that it has been agreed that public funding for those companies taking part in the civil Eureka programme, initiated by France, should be on an equal level to other European companies.

Also based on the 'technological leap forward' argument, the first projects under the Alvey programme were started in 1984. The programme was originally initiated to compete with the Japanese fifth-generation computer project, bringing together industry and universities and research institutes in co-operative programmes of pre-competitive research. Although originally envisaged to include all industry in the IT sector, the award of grants has been dependent on matching funding so has tended to exclude smaller firms. It has been criticised for its slow start-up, for allowing the entry of multinationals such as IBM, for its overemphasis on hardware, for its dependence on American operating software, and for the fact that pre-competitive research is the cheapest portion of innovation. In total, the government will spend £200 million over four years, but much of this comes from existing research budgets (*Hansard*, 12 March 1985, col. 92).

In its attempts to encourage the use of new technology the Thatcher government has spent £4·8 million specifically on equipping certain offices with showpiece office automation technology, although the equipment seems to have been imposed on the users rather than designed around their needs. The majority of support for innovation has come through the Microelectronics Applications Project (MAP), begun in 1978, and designed to spread the use of microelectronics in industry. The programme has been monitored by the independent Policy Studies Institute (1985) which found that companies which received MAP grants were measurably more successful in achieving microelectronics innovation than those which failed to attract government support. But it also criticised the time taken to approve grants — six months or longer — and the government's policy of insisting that a project could receive funding only if it were not to proceed without it. This precondition penalises go-ahead companies. (It also makes it easier, under other schemes for multinationals rather than national companies to fulfil the requirements). The government is also criticised for introducing a moratorium on spending early in 1985, justified on the basis that it had committed all the money allocated to the programme; stop — go strategies undermine confidence.

A further problem with the Support for Innovation strategy is that it does not link the programme of creating demand to market pull strategies. Hence, support under the robotics scheme was given to companies buying any make of robot and most that were bought came from Japan. At the same time as the only British maker of robots using British technology failed in 1982 for lack of a market, public funds went to Unimation (American controlled) for the importation of technology from Japan. In other programmes, as in MISP, public funds have gone without fuss to incoming multinationals. Yet the Anglo — American microchip company, Inmos, faced considerable difficulties in gaining public funding before it was sold to Thorn — EMI. Demands by manufacturing industry for public sector development contracts to develop British technology have been ignored by governments of both political parties.

There is considerable doubt, therefore, over the extent of technological innovation which is funded by government and the efficacy with which it is diffused or converted into exports for the civil market. An undue emphasis on large companies, which may use research and development contracts to boost short-term cash flow, and undue emphasis on defence electronics may have helped to weaken the British IT sector, And whilst Japan is strengthening the amount it spends on basic research, cuts in public expenditure in the UK, which have reduced the budgets of the Research Councils, have had the opposite effect. The privatisation of British Telecom seems also to have altered the emphasis of that organisation's research and development away from long-term to short-term profit-oriented research. The Trades Union Congress (TUC, 1985) has also pointed out the increasing dependence of the UK on research and development decisions taken overseas by multinational companies and the volatility of this short-term financing.

Legitimacy of IT
The trend within the IT sector is for it to become elitist, aligned with the privatisation of access and better services for the better-off. About 30 percent of British households do not have even a telephone. Following the privatisation of BT and its rebalancing of its tariffs, the up-front cost of telephone installation has risen to about £100 — more than one-quarter of monthly take-home pay, even for those on average

wages. Access to enhanced services such as Prestel, or to cable TV data banks have associated up-front costs with almost no provision for access or use by the general public.

There are the additional problems associated not only with job losses directly attributable to IT, but with changes in working conditions brought about by the technology and the increased control which it allows employers. In 1985 a MORI poll showed that there was more public support for computers to help children learn than for satellite or cable TV, and the majority were pessimistic about the job-creating benefits of new technology (the *Economist*, 14 September 1985). More than 40 percent expected that as a result of science and technology the rich would get richer and the poor poorer.

Current trends in IT policy do indeed seem set to increase job losses. Jim Northcott (1986, pp. 87–8) has found that the more firms introduce both products and process innovation, the more jobs are lost — that the previous argument that product innovation would lead to increased employment, offsetting the losses of process innovation, are not borne out. Others have also concluded that if European industry continues on its present growth path the result will be fewer jobs in IT-related work in the year 2000 than today, whilst both Japan and the USA increase their IT-related employment (Mackintosh, 1986).

Only if growth can be increased will there be an increase of jobs. Without that contribution to employment, it seems highly unlikely that the current acquiescence of trades unions in the application of the new technology can go on for ever. Current policy is set domestically to increase inequalities between those with access to the new technologies and those without, and internationally to increase inequalities between Japan, the USA and Europe.

DECLINE OR GROWTH

In a small domestic market the government's role as consumer is of immense importance, yet public purchasing of British industry's products has rarely been tied into development and has never been carried through into the whole of the public sector. For instance, it is not known how much of the current equipment in use in central government, local authorities, public corporations and universities is from British or European owned companies — this is information which was available in the 1960s.

The problem for European countries and for the British government is that national markets are too small to give the world market share which is estimated to be necessary for companies to benefit from large-scale production. A unified EEC market would, however, give this domestic market base. Because the European market is fragmented by national policies, the primary beneficiaries of the EEC as a regional trading bloc have been American multinationals because (a) they have been able under EEC regulations to be treated as domestic companies; (b) they have been able to utilise the EEC's pro-competition policy to challenge attempts by government to favour nationally owned companies; and (c) with the recession in Europe they have become increasingly important as employers.

In Europe 50 percent of IT production comes from foreign-owned companies and Europe imports more than 80 percent of the microchips which it uses. The European market is, therefore, not only fragmented by national policies, but also further fragmented by the introduction of products for multinationals competing with products of national companies. As markets have been liberalised so increasing proportions are taken by overseas company products as shown in trade statistics in relation to British telecommunications. Yet telecommunications in the rest of Europe remains under public control. With transmission now occupying a central place in marketing and information services, a public procurement policy towards European-owned industry within the EEC as a whole could ease the constraints of fragmented home markets. Some progress has already been made at an EEC level in research and development projects such as ESPRIT and RACE, in moves towards standardisation and in collaborative ventures between companies. But without market pull, it seems likely that growth will continue to fall behind both the American and Japanese industries. As large users increasingly call for an efficient trans-European transmission system, it seems that only by additional investment in infrastructure and in transmission projects to instigate market pull can the growth of the European IT industry and the British industry within Europe be assured. Without this investment the prospects are that the UK and Europe will decline further into offshore manufacturing sites and markets for American and Japanese companies, and the concept of the sovereignty of European nations will be even more problematic than it is today.

BIBLIOGRAPHY

ACARD (1980), *Information Technology*, HMSO, London.
Commission of the European Communities (1980), *Government Financing of Research & Development*, EEC, Brussels.

Council for Economic Priorities (1985), *The Strategic Defense Initiative: Costs, Contracts and Consequences*, CEP, Washington DC.
DES (1985), *New Technology and Mathematics*, HMSO, London.
DTI (1983, 1984, 1985), *Skill Shortages Report*, DTI, London.
DTI (1985, 1986), *Science and Technology Report*, DTI, London.
European Commission (1980), *Government Financing of Research and Development*, Brussels.
Finniston Report (1980), *Engineering Our Future*, Cmnd 7794, HMSO, London.
Hansard, 21 January 1985 col. 278; 12 March 1985, col. 92; 19 March 1985, col.
Hills, J. (1986), *Derequlation Telecoms*, Frances Pinter, London, and Westview, Colorado.
Loxley, G. (1980), *A Study of the Evolution of Concentration in the UK Data Processing Industry*. EEC, Brussels.
Mackintosh, I. (1986), *Sunrise Europe. The Dynamics of Information Technology*, Blackwell, Oxford.
Maddock, Sir Ieuan (1983), *Civil Exploitation of Defence Technology*, NEDC, London.
NEDC, Electronics EDC (1982), *Policy for the UK Information Technology Industry*, NEDO, London.
NEDC, Electronics EDC (1984), *Crisis Facing UK Information Technology*, NEDO, London.
Northcott, J. (1986), *Microelectronics in Industry. Promise and Performance*, PSI, London.
Northcott, J. et al. (1985), *Promoting Innovation: Microelectronics Application Projects*, PSI, London.
Prais, S. J., and Wagner, K., quoted in *Financial Times*, 23 May 1985.
TUC (1985), *The Future Business. Britain's R & D Crises*, TUC, London.

Managers and information technology

J. H. SMITH
University of Southampton

In studies of the introduction of information technology (IT), only limited attention has been paid so far to its implications for the work of managers. To some extent, this has resulted from an ingrained belief that technology is a factor which only arouses resistance from the rest of the labour force, but such a view has also been reinforced by research preferences in the relevant disciplines. If we look at academic research, there has been some significant progress, but there are major questions still remaining to be tackled.

In the UK, the study of technological change from a social science standpoint can be dated from the 1940s and classified as follows: (1) the analysis of sectoral shifts in employment attributed to technological change and having sociological implications, for example, for changes in class structure; (2) attempts to identify the sources of invention or innovation and the economic aspects of their exploitation; (3) studies of specific technologies and their implications for the relations between management and labour, with particular reference both to organisation structure and to worker resistance; and (4) studies of the role of science and technology within the political system, with particular reference to science policy.[1]

Until the mid-1970s, research into technological change was conducted on a modest scale, with limited support from government and private foundations, and within the boundaries of these separate categories. More recently the scene has changed dramatically, as in all mature industrial economies, with the advent of microprocessor-based technologies. For a variety of reasons, the challenge of 'new technology' has been widely proclaimed and a considerable range of research initiatives has been undertaken. Examples include the formation of the Technological Change Centre (with support from the Economic and Social Research Council (ESRC) and foundations) and the programme of the Joint Committee of the ESRC-SERC (Science and Engineering Research Council). Some useful survey material of a largely descriptive character has been published by the Policy Studies Institute, the Technical Change Centre and other bodies. An increasing number of detailed studies by university researchers of particular areas of employment such as printing, clerical work and the car industry and of particular technologies, such as Computer Numerical Centre (CNC), have begun to appear. Theoretical perspectives have been most apparent in work set in the context of the 'labour process' approach following Braverman, but attention has been given to devising a more comprehensive framework for the analysis of managerial behaviour in the implementation of change, for example managerial descretion, strategic coalitions. In addition, some studies have broke new ground in attempting to identify the relationship between, on the one hand products market change, managerial strategy and the adoption of process innovation; and, on the other, the impact on the nature of work and trades union responses.

Despite this increased sophistication and the generally high level of competence shown in these studies of new technology, they remain conceptually and analytically very much in the mould of the pioneering work of the 1950s and 1960s.[2] Particular defects are the absence of genuine interdisciplinary work and the over-simplified view of 'technology'; this is usually taken as a given, an uncritical starting point. In the New Technology Research Group, established at the University of Southampton in 1978, we in the Department of Sociology and Social Administration have attempted to confront these issues of interdisciplinary effort, by collaborating directly with engineers, and to define the challenges of new technology with greater precision.

The objectives of the group are to explore the process of technological change with particular reference to: the problems of engineering and management choice and design of new technologies in work organisations; the nature of strategies developed to implement new technologies in the work place, including education and training in new skills; the development of trades union strategies in response to the introduction of new technologies; the consequences of technological change for the design of work and attitudes of work groups; the effectiveness of industrial relations procedures in handling the issues arising from technological change; and the consequences of technological change for management, supversision and organisational structure.

The continuing aim is to provide an independent assessment and evaluation of the processes and issues raised by the introduction of new technologies.

Following feasibility studies funded by the University's Committee for Advanced studies, support by the ESRC/SERC Joint Committee enabled three longitudinal studies to be undertaken: the adoption of a computerised freight information system in British Rail; the introduction of electronic news gathering equipment in TV South; and telephone exchange modernisation in British Telecom (BT).[3]

We started on this research because we were involved in a new teaching programme for engineers, and felt we did not have enough up-to-date material. Technical change and its social implications was an obvious topic; there was a lot of material about 'old' technology (for example, in steel, coal, the car assembly line) and there was a lot about worker resistance. We felt we wanted some examples from electronics and electronics-based industry and our colleagues in the Department of Electronics were interested in participating. So we began to develop an interdisciplinary approach: this involved a long period of familiarisation in which we set out to understand each other's interests and each other's language. In the course of that period we agreed that we would embark on longitudinal studies where possible, focusing on the process of change rather than on single events. In particular we wanted to get away from the 'black box' version of technology: we wanted to analyse technology as a factor in greater depth, so that we could give more meaning to the notion of technological choice in the process of decision-making. Above all we wanted to get away (and we were greatly encouraged by our engineer colleagues in this) from monocausal explanations, so we tried to remain eclectic and open-minded. We looked at all the latest approaches, such as 'contingency theory', 'labour process theory' and 'strategic choice', and took note of what we found to be relevent and suggestive. However, we remained consistent in our view that we should look particularly closely at technology. In appraising the work that had been coming out in recent years, we came to the conclusion that the importance of technology itself had been down graded.

By the late 1970s, studies of change had tended to move away from so-called technological determinism and to discard 'technology' as a single explanatory variable. One view was that too much emphasis on technology promoted a kind of long-run fatalism; in particular, that if too much attention was paid to technology it suggested a kind of resignation to all sorts of unpleasant, but inevitable, outcomes, and especially net losses in human terms. There was, however, other work, more sceptical in its approach, which was seen as more optimistic (for example, Buchanan and Boddy 1983, Wilkinson 1983). This questioned the inevitability thesis but at the same time tended to relegate the technological variable in various ways. This was achieved by pointing up the social determinants of work tasks, worker attitudes, group practices, occupational traditions, and so on.

It was argued that these social factors deserved much more emphasis in assessing the real life situation in the workplace. Now this can be seen as one of those perfectly understandable swings of the pendulum, so often found in the longer running academic arguments. Theory should always be modified by practical experience and insights combined with contrary points of view. But we took the view that things had gone a bit too far and that there was a real risk of throwing the 'technological baby' out altogether in putting the case for social determinants.

Having said that, it proved difficult to find definitions of technology appropriate to the kind of workplace research that we ourselves wanted to conduct. This was the point at which we began to look closely at specific technologies and to see where an interdisciplinary approach might lead. One technological setting on which spent a great deal of time was the telephone exchange; the particular process of technological change we studied in this context was the transition from the old Strowger electromechanical set-up to the TXE4 semi-electronic or intermediate system — intermediate, that is, between the traditional form of exchange and the fully computerised type (BT's System X).[3]

Now most definitions of technology recognise different elements. These tend to be arranged in ascending levels of analysis, which get heavier and heavier and vaguer and vaguer. They all start more or less with specific items of equipment, apparatus or hardware, which for the participants must be the focus of changes in the jobs they do. But definitions can then move on to questions of process layout and workload process; next, to the level of the organisation, or simply work done in the organisation; then, perhaps even the idea of the organisation itself. At this point the level is so abstract that it provides no kind of research instrument for the study of technological change.

In our research we have tried to characterise technology in terms that allow for more precise measurement of its effect on work and its organisation. We start with the basic assumption that all technologies are engineering systems; in short, they are based on engineering principles and they are composed of elements functionally arranged in specific ways. We list three primary elements or inputs: these give the technology its distinctive form. First comes the system principles; second, the system configuration overall. Those two elements we call the architecture. The third primary element is the system implementation, i.e. the physical realisation of those principles and the configuration; system implementation is the technology in both the hardware and the software sense. It will of course, be evident that you cannot separate them totally; the architecture is not separate from the technology in any finite sense, but for analytical purposes this is the way we decided to proceed.

Having identified the three primary elements of the technology, we would argue that it is possible to have more than one implementation of a given basic architecture. Once it is acknowledged that it is possible to implement in more than one way, then you are in a position to talk about choice within a given technological framework. Conversely, standardised implementations of certain functions, for example, in electronics-based hardware and software, are to found in a wide variety of system architectures. So there are primary elements of architecture and technology, but there are also secondary elements. Here we move into the design space, as we called it, into the realm of 'dimensioning'. Dimensioning is the detailed design of the engineering system for a particular organisational setting; this is an area in which new thinking and new research are called for. We also identified as a secondary element what we call 'appearance'; this includes the audible and visible characteristics of the technology.

The element of appearance opens up questions of ergonomics and aesthetics. Our argument is that choices made about specific dimension — or the detailed design within an engineering system — can exert significant influences, for example, on the nature and experience of work from the point of view of the people who have to operate it. A further aspect which we think needs an increased emphasis in research of this kind, is the way in which a given physical implementation generates visible and audible characteristics. The direct result of the system architecture, these visible and audible characteristics are an important part of subjective work experience and changes in them need to be studied in their own right.

Now the system appearance, as we have called it, may have a direct bearing on work context and work experience. A simple illustration of this is given by the effects of moving from mechanical to electronic settings. This is shown by our work on the changeover in telephone exchanges from Strowger to TXE4. The Strowger system will be familiar to any Hitchcock fans who remember *Dial M for Murder* and perhaps its most dramatic scene. This is when a telephone call, part of a murder plot, is being made and there is a close-up of the step-by-step switching. If this film is ever remade in a modern setting they will have to find something quite different, because with electronic switching no mechanical movements are visible, you cannot actually see things going up and down or clicking. (Hitchcock would probably have introduced some sort of system fault, and there would have to have been an anxious period until a maintenance technician turned up to deal with it.) In the old Strowger system, the step-by-step switching is electromechanical; as it works it moves and it makes a noise — in fact, it rattles and clicks. You can see it and hear it moving up and down, and this provides aural and visual proof that it is, in fact, working. The TXE4 system is a telephone exchange system which is based on common control matrix switching and it is semi-electronic. It has few aural or visual indicators. Its components are hidden in racks of plug-in units and the common understanding of the maintenance function is the replacement of plug-in units. This enhances fault tolerance and more comprehensive automatic fault monitoring and reporting capabilities. The group studied eight exchanges, two Strowger, which remained as such; four conversions from start to finish, which moved all the way from Strowger to fully operational TXE4; and two conversions that had happened before our research. The methods of study used included: self-report diaries, that is, asking maintenance technicians to keep a daily diary sheet for twenty working days; formal taped interview with fifty-one technicians and supervisors; periods of observation; comprehensive documentation; and inverviews with key informants amongst managers and trade unionists.

BRITISH RAIL AND TOPS

As you will gather, our preferred method has been to study change as an ongoing process. An exception was the study we made in British Rail of the computerisation of freight management — the introduction of the TOPS (Total Operations Processing System) system. This was, in fact, a retrospective study for which we were provided with very good documentation and interviewing facilities.[4]

In the 1960s the economic problems experienced by British Rail (BR) in its freight operations became extremely severe. The rail freight business was under pressure due to growing competition from other forms of transport, and as a result of the decline of industries such as coal, iron and steel, which had most used rail for bulk traffic. In response to the concern expressed by government about the operating losses of the rail freight business, BR carried out a series of major planning exercises. Amongst other findings, the poor quality of service to the customer was identified as a major factor in the decline of the business.

This poor quality of service was largely a consequence of the slow, inaccurate and unreliable information available to local and headquarters management concerning the whereabouts of the wagon fleet day-to-day. It was apparent to BR management that one way of dealing with this problem, was to make use of the availability of new computing and data transmission technologies. This would enable improvements to be made to the speed and efficiency of the rail freight network and, it was hoped, halt the decline in the business. BR decided in 1971 to invest £13 million in a new computer system, TOPS, to control its freight operations. The system has been in operation since 1975 following a four-year implementation programme.

In 1971, BR's freight operations were based on a stock of over 600,000 wagons and 3,000 locomotives, travelling over several thousands of miles of track. It also involved thousands of staff working in marshalling yards, freight terminals and sidings throughout the UK. Before computerisation, management information relied on daily physical checks in these dispersed locations. The results of these checks were then collated manually and disseminated through a hierarchical reporting procedure. The problem was that it was impossible for headquarters management to check the accuracy of the information and, in any event, the information was largely out of date by the time they received it.

In these circumstances, computer information technology offered obvious benefits, including the collection of accurate information from geographically dispersed locations, plus the availability of this information in 'real time' to similarly dispersed locations. After exploring several options, including the possible development of an 'in-house' product, BR chose the TOPS system. TOPS was a modified version of a system pioneered by the Southern Pacific Railroad (SPR) in the USA, and developed collaboratively by SPR and IBM. The decision by BR to choose an already proven operational system had important implications for the subsequent implementation of TOPS in the UK.

Although buying an already proven system had significant advantages, BR still faced considerable technical and organisational problems in implementing TOPS. Failure to implement quickly carried the risk of large increases in costs. Also overshadowing the project was the uncertainty and risk that the decision to introduce TOPS would fail to halt the decline of the freight business. In view of the serious economic position of the business, it was decided that TOPS must be implemented within a four-year time scale and also within budget. This put a premium on ensuring that a substrategy for implementing TOPS was devised which could achieve those objectives.

The implementation of the TOPS system required the setting up of a nationwide network of reporting points at over 150 locations, all linked to a central computer in London. One of the lessons from the North American experience was the importance of keeping staff training 'in phase' with the installation of the technology itself. The implementation substrategy was as much about staff training as it was about technical matters.

The TOPS project had the highest level support from the chief executive of BR, who appointed a senior and well-respected manager to be in charge of the project team. Together, these two individuals devised a form of organisation for implementing TOPS that was unique in BR. The basic ingredient was the adoption of a 'task force' approach involving a project team deliverately constructed on cross-functional lines. The main purpose of this form of organisation was to overcome established interests and interdepartmental rivalries within the management structure of BR. The team comprised computer, telecommunications and operating specialists under the overall control of the senior operating manager. Since the latter reported directly to the chief executive, the project team had direct access to the ultimate authority in the organisation.

The choice of the senior operating manager as project team manager was especially important because it gave the team credibility in its dealings with the operating functions. Because of the scale of the implementation task, the project team decided to introduce the TOPS system into the network over a two-year period from August 1973 to September 1975. The procedure was that as each local area was 'cut over', i.e. linked into the system, the specialist implementation teams would move on to the next location. Like the overall project, the implementation teams were headed by managers with an operating background, to give credibility to the team.

The implementation substrategy was as much concerned, as already mentioned, with staff training. In line with the task force approach, training was carried out in old railway coaches used as travelling classrooms. This approach enabled the trainers to continue as implementers at each location and, thus, see the staff through the entire process of the changeover to the new computerised system. The process of taining was not merely a matter of giving staff the appropriate skills, but was also designed to engender a 'culture of change'. This was a reflection of the spirit of enthusiasm and commitment consciously generated in the project team. The outcome of the implementation substrategy was that TOPS was fully operational on time and within budget.

The decision substrategy for TOPS was shaped by various factors, including the nature of market changes, the worsening performance of the freight business, political pressure from government, and the availability of new computer and telecommunications technology. The choice of TOPS had implications in terms of the experience available elsewhere and the other benefits of an already proven system. The implmentation substrategy was partly shaped by the tight cost and time limits for the project imposed by BR, in the light of some of the factors shaping the decision substrategy. It was also shaped by the need to overcome established organisational structures and interests. The substrategy adopted involved a 'task force' approach and the creation of cross-functional project team responsible for all aspects of implementation. The substrategy also depended upon the creation of a 'culture of change' to substain the commitment to the project. It is important to point out that despite the success of the implementation substrategy, further unforeseen problems and opportunities arose follwing implementation. This point serves to emphasis both the nature of technological change as a process and the implications of information technology for management tasks as well as for the work routines of other employees.

CONCLUSIONS

In all our work we have tried to develop a stage approach rather than a simple before and after appraisal of the process of change. This raises a formidable set of questions for research methodology. For example, how you treat events in this kind of research and what actually constitutes an event. What is a critical juncture, what weight do you attach to the evidence of actors, particularly key actors? What we are currently trying to do is to link the characteristics of the engineering system to the perceptions of organisational change held by people in about twenty firms. What our study is highlighting is the way in which technological change is transforming the role of management itself and the characteristics of organisational structures.

Our research points to changes both in the nature of management activity and in the structures within which the managers operate. The common factor here is the process of control. Management is an activity designed to control resources — both human and material. Organisation structures are purposeful forms of control; they provide the means by which information about resources (what, how many, where) is made available and utilised to achieve objectives.

At the beginning of this century, Max Weber regarded the bureaucratic form of organisation as the most advanced expression of rationality in human affairs. The logic of control it embodies, based on specialist expertise, hierarchical progression and centralised authority has been the guiding principle of large-scale organisation in all industrial societies.

The basic technology of Weber's administrative system was primitive. The means of communication within and between levels were slow and cumbersome. This was especially the case in the transmission of any quantity of information. The rate and quality of information transmission was governed by human capacity, with the minimum in the way of mechanical aids. As we know, the computer and the development of office automation generally have transformed this situation. The principal consequences have been seen as: increased speed and volume of data provision; reduced labour costs; and changes in skill requirements.

These developments, significant though they are, leave out of consideration the radical effects on the traditional bureaucratic structure. All existing assumptions about structures of control, the location of specialisations within a hierarchy, the hierarchy itself are called in to question by the potential of computer applications. The distinction between management and organisation, always difficult to draw, becomes even more elusive, if by organisation we mean a form of communication and control by managers. Information and action can now be simultaneous.

In the early stage of the adoption of computers by large organisations, the possibility of conflict with traditional organisational forms was not seriously considered. On the whole, computers were seen as instruments which would reinforce centralised decision-making and exercise closer control by management over employees.

The growth of informal, end-user and personal computing has produced a strong countervailing tendency, with pressure for autonomy and initiative at what used to be regarded as the periphery of the large-scale organisation; but which is now undergoing a measure of redefinition. The reasons for this are partly economic (competitiveness, responsiveness), but they are also partly social and psychological (employee satisfaction, responsibility, potential for disruption).

My colleague Howard Rose and I have been exploring the nature of organisational changes in some twenty firms and have come to some preliminary conclusions about the changing place of computing systems within them. It appears from this work that the rapid growth in informal computing within organisations is creating a new version of an old organisational dilemma — the balance between centralisation and decentralisation and the location of specialists.[5]

Some of these questions have been addressed by Webb in a discussion of the growing demand within organisations for direct access to computing power and computerised information by users, including managers. The discussion by Webb focuses on five guidelines to managers to enable the redevelopment of flexible computing facilities.[6] The first guideline is to reduce the pressure on central mainframe facilities, which will continue to be required for formal data processing, by decentralising the facilities for informal computing. The second guideline urges managers to think in terms of networks rather than hierarchies which, he suggests, should make it easier to decide where to provide computing power in terms of the management of information within the network.

The significance of the need for organisations to deal with the servicing and management of informal computing is that the rapid growth of this activity and its inherent requirement for adaptability and fast response has meant that the traditional central computing facilities have been unable to provide an adequate service. The often unfortunate consequence has been the proliferation of a host of incompatible types of equipment and systems. The logic of the guidelines proposed by Webb is that the utilisation of technological developments can facilitate the decentralisation of much computing activity and reduce the dependence on mainframe systems. This, in turn, suggests the possibility of reassigning systems analysts who are no longer required for development work on formal systems to a support role for informal users. The implications of this are various. For example, it opens up the possibility of formally transferring systems analysts to user departments so that their allegiance is to those departments and they are carried on those departments' budgets. It raises the issue of how to provide the links between these user-dedicated specialists so that ideas are shared and work is not duplicated. It also raises the matter of the role of the central computing department and the extent to which it should control the overall development of computerisation.

In their different ways systems integration and end-user computing have contributed to the dilemma facing managers as they seek to find ways to manage computing services and systems. The issue may be posed in terms of a search for organisational forms which strike a balance between maintaining centralised control and providing decentralised facilities. Whilst this may not be a new problem for organisations, the rapid developments in the scale and range of computer applications now poses it in a new and acute form. Without wishing to press the point too hard, there is a similarity here to Peters and Waterman's discussion of 'loose-tight properties' in organisational structures.[7]

So far we have completed the study of six firms only, so what I have to say is tentative. These firms include manufacturers of electrical equipment, computer equipment, heating and ventilating systems and pharmaceuticals, a DIY retailer, and an insurance firm.

These firms can be placed somewhere on a continuum according to (1) the degree of centralisation or devolution of computing expertise; and (2) the extent and manner of control over computer developments and hardware and software standards. The greatest extremes appear to be found in (1), with centralisation at its maximum in the insurance firm and devolution greatest in the heating and ventilation manufacturer. The reasons for this seem clear enough. The primary tasks in insurance are basic, simple and readily standardised. In the heating and ventilation firm, design requirements call for greater flexibility; it was also the case that this firm had an unsatisfactory early experience with central computing facilities. But within these extremes, we are conscious that choice is being exercised and that the use of the new technology is shaped by the business objectives and previous experience of the enterprise. The crucial issues centre on the part played by individual decisions and preferences, and the capacity to reinterpret traditional managerial roles. These are the major challenges posed for management by the adoption of information technology and we in the New Technology Group will continue to explore them in our current programme. This revolution in managerial work is at least as great as any of the consequences of technological change for the rest of the labour force, in the longer term it promises to be the greatest and the most far-reaching.

REFERENCES

1 Studies of this type included:
Burns T., and Stalker G., (1961), *Management of Innovation*, Tavistock, London.
Carter, C. F., and Williams, B. R. (1957), *Industry and Technical Progress*, Oxford University Press, London.
Clark, C. (1947), *The Conditions of Economic Progress*, Oxford University Press, London.
Cole, G. D. H. (1955), *The Influence of Technological Change on the Class Structure of Western Europe*, Allen & Unwin, London.
Hunter, L. C. et al. (1969) *Labour problems of Technological Change*, University of Glasgow, Social and Economic Studies, New Series, 18.
Scott, W.H., (1956), *Technical Change and Industrial Relations*, Liverpool University Press, Liverpool.
Trist, E.L. et al. (1963), *Organisational Choice*, Tanistick, London.
Woodward, J. (1965), *Industrial Organisation: Theory and Practice*, Oxford University Press, London.

2 For example,
Buchanan, D. A., and Boddy, D. (1983), *Organisations in the New Computer Age*, Gower, Aldershot.
Child, J. (1984), *Organization: A Guide to Problems and Practice*. Harper & Row, New York.
Gallie, D. (1978), *In Search of the New Working Class*, Cambridge University Press, Cambridge.
Gershuny, J. (1983), *Social Innovation and the Division of Labour*, Frances Pinter, London.
Gershuny, J., and F. Miles, I. (1983), *New Service Economy*, Frances Pinter, London.
Knights, D. (ed.) (1985), *Job Redesign: Critical Perspectives in the Labour Process*, Gower, Aldershot.
Martin, R. (1981) *New Technology and Industrial Relations in Fleet Street*, Clarendon Press, Oxford.
Northcott, J. (1982), *Microelectronics in Industry: What's Happening in Britain*, Policy Studies Institute, London.
Pugh, D. S., and Hickson, D. J. (1976), *Orangisation Structure in its Context: the Aston Programme*, Saxon House, Farnborough.
Sorge, A. et al. (1983), *Microelectronics and Manpower in Manufacturing: Applications of Numerical Control in Great Britain and West Germany*, Gower, Aldershot.
Warner, M. (ed.) (1984), *Microprocessors, Manpower and Society*, Gower, Aldershot.
Wilkinson, B. (1983), *The Shopfloor Politics of New Technology*, Heinemann, London.
Willman, P., and Winch, G. (1984), *Making the Metro: Technological Change, Management Strategy and Industrial Relations at BL Cars*, Cambridge University Press, Cambridge.
Wood, S. (ed.) (1982), *The Degradation of Work? De-skilling and the Labour Process*, Hutchinson, London.

3 See the various reports of the New Technology Group summarised in the Annual Report for 1986. The full account of the BT study is published in Clark, J., King, R., McLoughlin, I. and Rose, H. (1987), *The Process of Technical Change: New*

Technology and Social Choice in the Workplace, Cambridge University Press, Cambridge.
4 McLoughlin, I., Smith, J. H., and Dawson, P. (1983), *The Introduction of a Computerised Freight Information System in British Rail*, NTRG Report.
5 See H. Rose and J. H. Smith, 'The organisational challenge of new engineering systems', in C. A. Voss (ed.) (1986), *Managing Advanced Manufacturing Technology*; H. J. Rose, 'Constructing Organisational Forms for Flexible Computing', papers presented to workshop on the Implications of Information Technology for the Role of Management and Management Development (Brussels, 1986). The passage which follows is taken from this paper.
6 Webb, T. (1985), 'Towards more flexible computing?', *Management Services*.
7 Peters, T. J., Waterman, R. H. (1982), *In Search of Excellence: Lessons from America's Best-run Companies*, Harper & Row, New York.

Technological innovation and education – the case of the microcomputer

RAINER RUGE
Federal Republic of Germany

Computing is the technology that drives all other technologies.
[Feigenbaum and McCorduck, 1984, p. XVII]

Technology by itself is not the solution, but lack of it is part of the problem.
[Ager, 1983, p. 9]

The computer is a Rohrschach ink blot test for educational philosophy. The computer is so versatile, so rich in possibilities, that virtually any view of what education is or ought to be can be implemented on it.
[ETC, 1984, p. 8]

INTRODUCTION

The advent of the microcomputer or personal computer (PC) is just beginning to have a marked impact on advanced industrialised societies, especially the USA, Japan and some Western European countries. What is new? For the first time the computer, having shrunk in size and gained in power, *ceteris paribus*, is to be found beyond such highly specialised fields as large-scale number crunching or handling very large data sets.

The microprocessor, virtually a computer *en miniature*, and the microcomputer have become so small, potent, and relatively inexpensive (with a lot more cost-cutting just around the corner) that they are on the brink of becoming ubiquitous in what Ralf Dahrendorf aptly called the 'OECD World'. Microprocessors control household appliances and car engines, not to mention aeroplanes and public transit systems; they are to be found in gardening devices and in children's toys; they please the audiophile; and, in an automatic teller machine, the after hours customers. Likewise, the small microcomputer is in the process of penetrating industrialised societies at a pace which was inconceivable only five or eight years ago. The smallest and less sophisticated versions populate children's rooms; students as well as supermarket managers or farmers use (and own) one, with office workers, professionals and academics leading the way into the 'compunications' age.[1]

This anecdotal evidence was chosen with the thrust as well as the spread of the 'digital way' in mind. The very fast and dramatic 'digital evolution' of the last two decades (and the forty or so years of data present before this) are likely to affect the fabric of advanced industrial societies as deeply as other major technological advances – the steam engine, the printing press, the railroads and the automobile – have done in the past. Some even compare the likely impact to the invention of the alphabet and the transition from oral to written record.[2]

Digital processes, the devices for handling them and the uses to which they are put make up a complex 'bundle' which people are only gradually beginning to understand. The Harvard Information Business Map, as developed by the Program on Information Resources Policy, is a first and rather powerful attempt to construct a conceptual map. It has been used by Oettinger (1984) to clarify the evolution of telecommunications in the USA, and has the digital processor (or computer) right at the centre. The choice seems justified because, 'the greater versatility, precision, reliability, abundance and low cost of electro-optical digital formats are the practical keys to unlocking the vast and versatile powers of electro-optical digital processes' (Oettinger, 1984, Chapter 3, p. 39). If this is indeed so, as I will assume, then the digital programmable multi purpose processor (or computer, for short) is not just a gadget that will soon fade away. The microcomputer is the outgrowth of a (*the?*) core technology of our time, making the technology available almost everywhere and for an incredible variety for purposes.[3]

Any radically new technology which is also a core technology poses a challenge to the society which engenders it. It triggers a demand for learning as it penetrates the world of work and people's *Lebenswelt* at large. Depending on the evolution of the technology and on its rate of penetration, a long span of time may elapse before a new technology gets firmly established in a society. Clanchy (1979), for example, presents an interesting case history on the transition from memory to written records in the UK since the twelfth century. In this transition period a growing number of adult members of society require education and training with respect to the new technology. As it finally becomes more established, acquiring related skills becomes part and parcel of socialisation. Adults are, at the same time, likely to be working towards more enhanced technology-related skills or competencies. These were, as Clanchy has shown, highly sophisticated and differentiated depending on the type of document. The rate of penetration has accelerated markedly in recent history. It is quite high at present, largely due to advances in transportation and communication technologies; non-joiners do not survive.

Such demand for learning often exists in informal settings, but formal learning processes take place within the confines of a well-defined education system in society. The education system and organised learning processes have grown considerably over time in terms of importance and scope. They are likely to grow even further where post-industrial, knowledge-based societies emerge (Bell, 1973; Feigenbaum and McCorduck, 1984).

It is the aim of this chapter to look at the new technology, the microcomputer, and at the education system from a policy-making perspective, exploring impacts, interrelationships and feedbacks. I will look at history and contemporary examples, and also explore the problems of functional and computer literacy.

AN HISTORICAL DIGRESSION: THE PRINTING PRESS AND OTHER AGENTS OF CHANGE

The subject of microelectronics in the literature, especially in its more popular branches, abounds with sweeping historical generalisations and ill-conceived analogies. Yet historical comparisons may serve at least three useful purposes: they may, by raising 'what if' questions, stimulate the investigator's hypothesis-generating imagination; some outcomes or side-effects of earlier innovations may, indeed, be very similar to those of present day innovations, so that quite direct inferences are warranted; and finally, the exploration of historical analogies may help to create a larger framework for understanding technology-stimulated social change. Compaine (1984) and Oettinger (1984) illustrate the various uses of history for the exploration of modern digital technology quite well.

Francis Bacon's well-known and aften quoted Aphorism has set the tone for much enquiry:

> We should note the force, effect, and consequences of inventions which are nowhere more conspicuous than in those three which were unknown to the ancients, namely, printing, gunpowder, and the compass. For these three have changed the appearance and the state of the whole world...
> [*Novum Organum*, Aphorism 129]

This triad has, of course, been disputed. In the view of Braudel, the eminent French historian, 'only ocean navigation ended by creating any upheaval or asymmetry in the world' (quoted and disputed by Eisenstein, 1979, p. 27). Ocean navigation did not only depend on the compass, it also depended on a fairly accurate determination of the longitude at sea which presupposed one of the pivotal high technologies of modern times, as David Landes has shown (1983); namely the exact measurement of time. Clocks have helped to make long-distance navigation a viable commercial enterprise, transforming the world (as Braudel had indicated). But clocks have also been intimately linked to advances in physics and astronomy. And they have, finally, contributed to shaping modern social structures in a way hard to overrate by dividing up the time-continuum and allowing an unprecedented co-ordination among members of society.

The printing press, so it has been argued by Eisenstein (1979), must also be seen as a first-order technological innovation.[4] The printing press is a particularly interesting technological innovation since it too is an example of what Daniel Bell has called an 'intellectual technology' (see Forester, 1981, p. 503).

Printing 'revolutionised all forms of learning', or, in the words of a historian quoted by Eisenstein (1979, pp. 3, 28)

> The invention and development of printing with movable type brought about the most radical transformation in the conditions of intellectual life in the history of western civilisation. It opened new horizons in education and in the communication of ideas. Its effects were sooner or later felt in every department of human activity.
> [Gilmore, 1952, p. 186]

The staggering change in scale implied by the new technology is well highlighted by Clapham (1957, p. 37):

> A man born in 1453, the year of the fall of Constantinople, could look back from his fiftieth year on a lifetime in which about eight million

books had been printed, more perhaps than all the scribes of Europe had produced since Constantine founded his city in AD 330.[5]

Following Eisenstein (1979, p. 71, ff.), a number of effects on printing can be identified which look surprisingly modern; they seem well-suited to guide the imagination in an exploration of the digital evolution of the twentieth century.

First, increased output led to altered intake. The sixteenth century experienced a knowledge explosion, perhaps not unlike that of the twentieth century. Few contemporary writers failed to point out the excitement and abundance of the new bookish knowledge, 'all the world is full of learned men ... of vast libraries ... neither of Plato's time, nor in Cicero's was there ever such opportunity for studying ...' (Rabelais). No longer was it necessary to be a wandering scholar in order to consult different books. The new wealth of ideas and information which was becoming available made it more difficult to reconcile divergent traditions. But it also challenged people to try their wits at unscrambling the scrambled data that was presented to them. It should be noted that the technological innovation created a new intellectual centre: the print workshop. The workshops were often set up and run by scholar printers whose reputation frequently outstripped that of colleges and universities, and who combined, in a quite novel way, empirical and theoretical competencies.

Second, printing brought about unprecedented standardisation. Before, in the age of the scribe, it had been nearly impossible to produce identical copies. Identical images especially were virtually impossible to replicate by hand. But printing also enchanced standardisation in a more substantive way, by making calendars, dictionaries, ephemerides and other reference guides as well as maps, charts, diagrams and other visual aids widely available. But standardisation also bred a new altertness to the individual and the diverse. If it was possible to reproduce, say, pictures of costumes with a high degree of precision, the possibility for imitation (and, thus, the spreading of fashions) and the perception of difference had been opened up.

Third, reorganising texts and reference guides for printing had profound effects on rationalising, codifying and cataloging of data and knowledge. It may seem amazing but it was only then that such apparently trivial skills as alphabetical ordering became the norm, as placing letters in alphabetically ordered piles became a routine task in the printer's workshop. Similarly, indexing made a breakthrough with the advent of printing. On a more elaborate level, printing spurred the advance of logical scrutiny and of intellectual analysis. All conceivable topics began to be explored by encyclopedic works, 'on the method of ... '; thus, the modern textbook was born, the writing of which was made profitable by the printing press. Furthermore, scholars could explore the logic of texts that had now become available in their entirety for the first time. As Eisenstein (1979, p. 103) points out, 'very few teachers on [medieval] law faculties had a chance to see the *Corpus Juris* as a whole'; hence they could not be, and were not, very concerned with the relationships among the various parts of the *Corpus* or between the parts and the whole. The Florentine Codex, at Pisa, for example, was not easily accessible even to scholars.

Fourth, the technology that made the production of identical copies possible also paved the way towards the emendation of texts, thus introducing the idea of feedback into the intellectual enterprise in a quite unprecedented sense. It was the fixity of the printed text which made substantial improvements possible, not only by compiling lists of *errata* and by correcting subsequent printings, but, more importantly, by building up, through books and scientific collaboration vast treasure houses of factual information. Topography, botany and zoology furnish telling examples. Early modern astronomy is further testimony to the importance of improved communication among researchers, of an increasing wealth in observational data, and of facilitating more accurate observations now by 'stationary' scholars while the books circulated.

Fifth, the preservative powers of print need to be stressed. 'Steady advance', as Sarton put it, 'implies the exact determination of every previous step', an intellectual feat impossible to achieve before printing (Eisenstein, 1979, p. 124). And a feat with remarkable social consequences: the body of laws became more susceptible of scrutiny; the battle over precedents became more important because departure from them became more difficult. Religious division apparently became more permanent due to the fixity of the printed word. The rise of printing created the need for a legal definition of intellectual property rights and, conversely, forced a legal definition of what belonged in the public sphere.

Sixth, and last, printing contributed to a far-reaching social transformation: the reading public it created was more dispersed and individualistic than the hearing public. The less volatile medium – print compared with speech – also encouraged interest, and even vicarious participation, in more distant events. Causes could win followers that had no advocate in the local community. Hence, printing, with its implied stress on individual authorship, not only undermined the older form of collective authority, but also helped to shape new forms of group identity.

I do not wish to dwell on the historical analogies in any detail, but rather to suggest their use to highlight problems of contemporary high technology. It is obvious that the more hidden, basic and far-reaching consequences of a new technology are also the more interesting and difficult ones to investigate. The rise of alphabetical ordering is a good case; can structurally analogous consequences be identified for the 'digital way'? It is to much simpler questions that we now turn, bearing in mind that our topic is not the social consequences of the microcomputer *per se*, but rather its consequences for education, the education system, and educational policy-making.

COMPUTER-AIDED INSTRUCTION: THEN AND NOW

Scholars investigating the social impact of major technological innovations have, more often than not, been carried away by that particular innovation. Researchers on, and advocates of, computer-aided instruction (CAI) are no exception to this rule.

> One can predict that in a few more years millions of school children will have access to what Philip of Macedon's son Alexander enjoyed as a royal prerogative: the personal services of a tutor as well-informed and responsive as Aristotle.
> [Suppes, 1966, p. 207]

> *Computer Centred Learning* offers the first real opportunity for individualising the educational experience of millions of children ... As a direct teaching and learning tool, the computer offers the likelihood – over the next decade or two – of making learning an exciting and welcome experience for *every child* in the school system.
> [Technomics, Inc[6]]

Or a more recent voice: the computer is 'perhaps the most exciting potential source of educational improvement in centuries' (Lesgold and Reif, 1983, p. III).

While there has been much indulgence in untested potential and a lot of grand rhetoric, critical scrutiny of CAI claims has been a commodity in desperately short supply. A notable exception is Oettinger (1969). The book poses a number of searching questions which even today, nearly twenty years later after much further CAI work and a most dramatic evolution in computer technology, are as fresh and relevant as they were then. Oettinger focuses on three sets of problems with respect to computers in education: (i) cost and amount: how many computers or computer workplaces are we going to need in order to make optimal use of the new technology in education? What outlays will be required? How do they compare with present and future educational budgets?; (ii) reliability and maintenance: this aspect of educational innovation – the ever recurring story of last year's gadget sitting in some cupboard gathering dust because something broke and spare parts are no longer available or funds for repairs are not in the school budget etc. – is dealt with in great and vivid detail (see especially Appendix B, p. 283 ff.); (iii) complexity, standardisation, integration and content: even if a particular piece of educational technology is affordable and works, it still must fit into the educational scheme. Is the technology not too complex to be handled by the teacher in a classroom setting? Is it standardised enough to allow for easy transportation of teaching materials? Can they be modified and adapted without too much difficulty to suit the learner's, the school's or the teacher's special needs? How well is the technology integrated with other key aspects of the educational process; does it, for example, enhance or block the development of social skills, or the interaction with other learners or with the teacher? And, most important of all, what content does the technology convey? How well does it support the major educational goals?

These questions were raised before the more recent advances in microchip technology made the microcomputer possible and sent prices tumbling down. The first computers suitable for CAI were smaller mainframes that cost about US$ 300,000, whereas today's at US$ 1,000 are fit for a wide range of CAI used (but by no means for all of those which must be deemed to have a large educational potential, networking, for example – see Lesgold and Reif, 1983, p. 2). The spectacular drop in price has considerably eased the financial problem of CAI. Purchases of the order of magnitude now required for getting started with CAI are much more within the reach of a school, a school system or a university than was the case one or two decades ago. With lower prices and a large number of parents and students among the buyers, a new consumer-driven dynamics has emerged. This is not to say that the high-flying goals – a microcomputer for every fourteen secondary school students by 1990 (Fiske, 1984) – might not turn out to be unattainable with the disposable resources for education. Yet financial constraints no longer seem to be the most formidable stumbling blocks on the path to an educational utopia as envisaged by Suppes and others.

Reliability and maintenance pose problems that are likely to be long-term. At present they attract less publicity because microcomputers have been with us for a relatively short while, especially in educational settings. The mismarriage of chewing gum and keyboard is not likely to pose a very serious problem to educational innovation, and perhaps less so as micros are becoming more widespread and more of a part of everyday experience thus reducing the challenge to tamper with them. The technology of micro computers is ill-suited to use under rough conditions; a floppy disk which has Coke spilt over it compares quite unfavourably with a book meeting the same fate. Neverthless, the real challenge of maintenance seems to lie in the extraordinary dynamic of the technological evolution in the microcomputer field, which leads to all sorts of incompatibilities. Clever programs that will not run on the machines available and the maintenance of yesterday's software gobble up a good deal of energy and enthusiasm in educational microcomputing.

Yet the problems of affordability, reliability and maintenance look tiny with respect to those of content and integration of the computer in the curriculum. Tryg Ager, a researcher at Stanford, claims that, 'courses taught by computer can be both academically adequate and instructionally appropriate' (1983, p. 6). Ager supports his bold view of CAI in the Suppes tradition – the computer does not so much aid, but rather takes over completely – by pointing out a number of courses of this kind (in elementary symbolic logic, mathematics, programming, elementary French, Russian and Armenian). But he hastens to add that, 'achievement of adequacy and appropriateness for a broad range of subjects is well beyond our grasp'. It is interesting to note the caveats put forth by as fervent an advocate of CAI as Ager:

> There are things that CAI does not do well, and which, if nevertheless implemented, might damage students. The skill of efficiently assimilating information by reading, the ability to formulate independent judgements, and the mastery of the art of rational conversation, are essential to the process of higher education and also general goals of the enterprise. To the extent that CAI in universities deters the development or diminishes the exercise of these skills, I believe it can be dehumanising. [Ager, 1983, p. 5]

Another danger is the compromising of the intellectual integrity of subject matter in CAI.

> It does not follow from the fact that a discipline, say chemistry, acquires a powerful new tool, that the tool can become the teacher. [Ager, 1983, pp. 5–6]

Whatever the nature of the limits of CAI, there is general consensus, and Ager voices it quite clearly, 'that sophisticated teaching software is not available; the production of such software is not well understood, and the achievement of wide enough use to justify initial investment is not likely' (p. 7).

If, however, software is the bottleneck, then attempts to remedy this state of affairs certainly merit scrutiny. The problem is both scarcity and abundance. As the microcomputer has developed in the last couple of years, the market for software has exploded, and so has the market segment for educational software, there having been an estimated 1 million microcomputers in USA schools in 1985 (Fiske, 1984). The *New York Times* reported that some 7,000 educational packages had been put onto the market by the spring of 1985 and that 100–150 new packages are being added each month. But only a tiny of those programes can be deemed first rate (Schmidt, 1985). The reason for this may well be that we are still lacking a deeper understanding of how to integrate microcomputer uses with a wide variety of learning processes and curricula.

It is the goal of Harvard's Educational Technology Center, among others, to furnish such knowledge and understanding. Recent research signals a decisive turning point in the creation of educational microcomputer software, leading the way to pedagogy-driven software development (ETC, 1984). The starting points are, 'targets of difficulty' viewed as 'a kind of cognitive or developmental obstacle, which if not removed from the learner's path, will impede further progress (ETC, 1984, p. 16). The center's research agenda identifies a number of them in the school's physics, mathematics and computer science curricula (one example is the confusion of heat and temperature). The outlined projects will explore ways of using the computer to master these obstacles. (It is worth mentioning that the center will also investigate the educational potential of other emerging information technologies such as the interactive videodisc or speech recognition and access to microcomputers. New frontiers for educational applications of computers are thus gradually becoming visible.) But the core of CAI will be drill and practice; tutorials; games and simulations; and using the computer as a tool or a tool maker, i.e. programming as well as tapping spreadsheets, data bases and word processing for education. In an old-fashioned and narrow sense, CAI refers to using the computer as a 'medium' (ETC, 1984, p. 6) or 'instrument' (Oettinger, 1969, p. 15) for passively absorbing some subject matter; the computer functions quite often as nothing but an expensive page-turner. In the as yet ill-explored 'intelligence' CAI, – ETC's ICAI – (ETC, 1984, p.

13) the *learning requires putting the computer to some active or creative use*. Oettinger (1969, p. 21), aptly speaks of the computer as an 'actor'. The two kinds of CAI form a remarkable contrast: in the 'old' CAI learning is directed learning, and the underlying psychology is Skinnerian; in ICAI, on the other hand, learning can be open learning (it can, of course, also be directed learning), and the underlying psychology is largely Piagetian.

Development in the CAI field has been spurred by technological advances and their economic consequences: reductions in costs and cuts in price.[7] The second order consequence of this development is the new technology's pervasiveness which, in turn, makes widespread CAI (or ICAI) both feasible and highly desirable. It is feasible because microcomputer hardware and educational software are becoming more and more easily accessible, to students, teachers, parents (who are spending five and a half times as much on educational programs as schools, according to Schmidt, 1985) and other learners.[8] And today's microcomputer is so much more potent (or will be in the foreseeable future) – memory size, processing speed, screen resolution, colour, graphics, communications and AI capabilities, the icon-type user-friendly interface are just a few examples – and, hence, much more educationally useful than its large CAI predecessor. At the same time, as microcomputers (and their more powerful kin) are penetrating the world of work at an ever increasing speed, competence with respect to computers is becoming an integral part of job-related competencies for more and more jobs. Compaine (1984, p. 40) has some telling evidence from the 'want ads' carried by the *New York Times*. A wide variety of quite different computer-related skills is beginning to be viewed as something a sound education cannot do without. It is obvious, however, that the set of computer-related skills to be acquired by the learner can only be specified with respect to the level and content of a course of study; the computer skills taught to a junior high school student or to a graduate student of engineering are as different as the rest of the subject matter they are being exposed to.

COMPUTER LITERACY: FUNCTIONAL LITERACY FOR THE COMPUTER AGE?

Preparing students for a world, especially a world of work, where computers are plentiful, has sometimes been referred to as making them computer 'literate'. The notion of computer literacy seems intuitively plausible. A quotation from Charles Dickens's novel *Bleak House* may serve to elucidate the point: Jo, an illiterate sweep shuffling through the streets of London, is utterly ignorant:

> as to the meaning of those mysterious symbols, so abundant over the shops and the corner of streets, and on the doors, and in the windows! To see people read, and to see people write, and to see the postman deliver letters, and not to have the least idea of all that language – to be, to every scrap of it, stone blind and dumb! It must be very puzzling ... to think (for perhaps Jo does think, at odd times) what does it all mean, and if it means anything to anybody to anybody, how comes it that it means nothing to me?[9]

Who would want themselves or their children to be left behind facing the arrival of the brave new computer world? A computer literacy craze is sweeping Western nations, driven, above all, by hysterical parents and educators, as well as by computer salespeople. Many of the claims of computer literacy programs seem to falter under probing. Noble (1984) has assembled, and exploded, a number of basic computer literacy claims. First, in the home or as a consumer, there will be no more of a need to be computer literate in order to cope than there is presently a need to be an auto or television serviceman to use a car or watch TV.

Second, with respect to schools, Noble (himself a teacher) embraces a somewhat ambivalent position. On the one hand, he claims that most courseware is of very low quality and practically useless – a view held by many educators. On the other, he is awaiting tomorrow's software which allegedly is so user friendly that neither students nor teachers require any computer literacy in order to run it.

Third, he says that even as a preparation for jobs computer literacy makes no sense, because many jobs will continue to involve either no computers at all or a low level of computer use that can be learnt easily within a week or two of practical instruction. Noble and other critics see some sinister scheme in all the clamour for computer literacy, perhaps a credential barrier widening gaps between social groups. It may also be simply a way to sell computers, or a way of making people more computer friendly and thus thwart a critical discussion of the social impact of computers.

CONCLUSION AND POLICY ISSUES

It is very appropriate, especially in a democratic society, to press for a public debate on crucial issues affecting every citizen and possibly the very fabric of society. Yet fear is no good counsel, nor is excessive simplification of problems.

Both are to be expected *vis-à-vis* the quite unprecedented challenge of the 'digital way'. The competencies required by an individual to function successfully in an information society, characterised by a ubiquity of electro-optical processes, are only just starting to become visible. Compaine (1984), in a cogent essay, has dubbed these competencies the 'new literacy'. Small wonder that the new literacy does not present itself clearly before our eyes with all its implications and consequences.

Compaine and Oettinger are suggesting a framework for the study of information processes in society which allows us to ask quite novel questions. Putting a technical innovation into a grand historical context and asking questions such as the following should be helpful for researchers and policy-makers alike: how does the power of digital information processing make fresh approaches to using information 'substance' possible?; is the way in which we use writing being restructed dramatically?; where are today's 'unthinkables' made feasible by the microcomputers? So far, the answers provided seem somewhat elusive; the questions are the real challenge. This is also the message of a closely argued report by Derek Bok (1985), the President of Harvard University.

There is however, general consensus on some fundamental points. As 'compunications' technologies (with the microprocessor and the microcomputer right at the centre) are evolving, they will continue to have a marked, probably increasing, impact on the world of work. The rapid technological change is likely to affect the character of jobs; more or less continuous learning and training efforts will be required of any worker (manual, clerical, or professional) and of any firm.[10] Hence, a fully fledged information society will also have to be a 'learning society', to borrow Torsten Husen's term. This is to say nothing of all of those learning efforts which are driven by social and cultural change in the wake of 'compunications' technology.

As a consequence of the new technology, the demand for education and training will rise in society; and so will the supply because the microcomputer is on the brink of becoming a powerful instructional device.[11] But we are not quite there yet. The available hardware is deemed inadequate by many experts, and so is the software. Scholars and developers agree that, today, education microcomputing is still seriously flawed. To put it in the words of Bill Ship, director of the Institute for Research in Information and Scholarship (IRIS) at

Brown University, 'we still don't quite understand yet what it is that scholars need' (Hermeren, 1987, p. 47); or, in the words of Adeline Naiman who is a software developer, 'few programs even begin to use the power of the computer' (Naiman, 1987, p. 198). Nevertheless, it is beginning to make sense to talk about the enormous potential of the new technology for education if it is used wisely. The potential of the new technology, so it seems, can be realised in almost all departments of the educational enterprise; certainly in the three major branches (schools, colleges and universities), and vocational and recurrent education and training may also benefit substantially from the evolution of instructional computing.

The benefits will accrue if, and only if, standardisation allows portability of software and in consequence, makes the development of educational software a viable enterprise; if the performance of microcomputers put to educational uses can be raised considerably; and if, last but not least, enough stimulating instructional software is forthcoming.[12] There is, however, no convincing reason why these goals should be beyond the reach of engineers and educators.

Some general conclusions regarding the potential of instructional microcomputing seem warranted. First, substantial benefits may derive from *individualising* the student's learning experience. Microcomputer-aided learning makes for flexibility. The choice of place and time is the student's. CAI is also self-paced which will help the slow or shy learner (who may fear exposure in the classroom) as there is ample opportunity for revision. Indeed, as the concept of 'mastery learning' suggests, CAI may be designed in such a manner as to make the students perform more or less perfectly before they can pass the final test.[13] The idea is that everyone is learning everything well, or, as Bork (1987, p. 204) puts it, 'mastery learning is the application of democracy to education'. Even if complete mastery is not reached, well-designed CAI provides for an especially intensive learning experience, because the technology facilitates and encourages interaction among students and between teacher and student.[14] Consequently, there is a particularly strong case for CAI as enrichment of other forms of teaching and learning.

Second, the development of educational courseware requires a deeper understanding of human thinking and human cognition. For it is quite obvious that without such deeper understanding little can be expected of using the microcomputer in education. If, however, cognitive science and related disciplines make major advances, quite novel learning environments may result. But until this has been achieved there can only be a vision starting from the assumption that the gist of all non-routine computer use within education and outside is, 'stretching the human reason and intuition, as telescopes and microscopes have extended human vision' (Oettinger, 1969, p. 36). The challenge is, enabling students, 'to take charge of the computer' (ETC, 1984, p. 13), not as clerical data processors do, but as scientists and engineers do:

> We may have some difficulty at present in imagining how we can use such a tool or what it will mean for our lives. Yet it is likely that a generation from now every educated person will consider a procedural approach to problem solving of all sorts natural and commonplace, will be comfortable with many strategies for structuring data and representing knowledge, and will regularly create unique tools for applying these strategies.
> [ETC 1984, p. 8]

Third, more and more frequently a merger of job-related education and work is to be observed. As more and more workers will be using computers in their work, a new form of CAI – embedded instruction – is making its headway utilising those microcomputers and computer terminals that are already sitting on people's desks in offices and workshops.[15] The new technology thus both facilitates and necessitates a perpetual overhaul of manual, clerical and professional workers' vocational skill and competencies. Embedded instruction can be seen as part of an unprecedented and powerful learning environment which is permeating information societies. Similarly, we may encounter a shift from a teacher or curriculum-dominated learning to a 'learning on demand' where the student's needs dominate and rich knowledge bases (yet to be created) will be tapped for education and training.

Fourth, some advocates of educational microcomputing view it as a means for bringing the costs of education down, or of overcoming a shortage of qualified teachers, trainers or other educators. The basic idea is that with the help of the new technology, more education can be delivered to a larger audience without lowering the quality. The case seems strongest for firms wanting to reduce the time their employees are away from work. Otherwise, it is too early to judge the economics of CAI: there may be savings, but large expenses will have to be incurred in order to procure the hardware and software.

The potential of the new technology for education, learning and training is quite extraordinary. The market dynamics driving the evolution of microcomputer technology will, most likely, be insufficient to realise fully the microcomputer's educational potential. Government action could promote educational microcomputing in several important ways: by supporting research and development in order to demonstrate the feasibility and to keep costs down; by supporting the evaluation and monitoring of educational software and hardware to keep junk out; by wisely making use of the new technology in government and related institutions for example, State schools, universities or in-service training; and, most importantly, by safeguarding equity with respect to the new technology in education.

REFERENCES

The views expressed are those of the author and do not necessarily reflect those of the West German Ministry for Education and Science.

1. The term was coined by Professor Oettinger, of Harvard; the idea behind it – that computing and communications processes have become virtually indistinguishable and should be perceived as one 'bundle' – is now generally accepted. (See also Bell in Forester, 1981, p. 514; Oettinger, 1984). See also Forester (1981, p. 25), 'Indeed computer and communications technologies have become so similar and intertwined that they are difficult to distinguish'. (Aberson and Hammond) – The French speak of *information* and *télématique* to denote the same thing.
2. See Compaine (1984); Forester (1981), pt III.
3. I have added the prefix to make it quite clear what kind of computers will be dealt with in the chapter.
4. Clanchy (1979) has drawn attention to the interesting point that 'printing succeeded because literate public already existed' (p. 1).
5. The quotation which I owe to Eisenstein (1979, p. 45) is from Clapham (1957, p. 37).
6. Both quotations are from Oettinger (1969, pp. 178 and 180).
7. For details see, for example, Forester (1981), chs 1 – 2; OTA (1983), chs 3 – 5.
8. Greater accessibility of microcomputers is the general trend. This is not to deny the serious problem of equity which receives a great deal of attention among responsible researchers. See for example ETC (1984, pp. 68, 70–1).
9. I owe this quotation to Feigenbaum and McCorduck (1984, p. 47).
10. For ample evidence see Gottlieb Duttweiler Institute (ed. 1987), especially the papers by Fisher, Hawkridge, Markus and Melmed.
11. Add-ons of various sorts, such as videodisks, all depend on the microcomputer to become educationally powerful. This even holds for networks and telelearning.
12. See especially the articles by Turner, Osgood (1987); Naiman (1987); Bork (1987) and the papers of the Joint Research Project on Computing in Educational Environment at Brown University, RI, USA and Lund University, Sweden.
13. Bork (1987, p. 202) quotes a physics course from the University of California at Irvine as an example.
14. The examples given are various – in a classroom only one student can give a certain answer or put forward an argument (and be original at the same time); not so on

a computer network. On a computer-taught course at Standford, 'The detailed feedback to the student is far superior to that provided in most lecture-based logic courses' (Bork, 1987, p. 202). On Brown University's Intermedia framework in which documents, graphics, video, sound and so on (all relating to one topic) can be created and linked, 'In one experimental religious studies class, students are submitting their papers online. The instructor links his comments to them and creates links among the student's papers, pointing out different approaches to the same argument' (Osgood, 1987, p. 178).

15 See Gottlieb Duttweiler Institute (ed. 1987), *passim*.

BIBLIOGRAPHY

Ager, Tryg A. (1983), *Problems and Possibilities of Computer-Aided Instruction*, Mimeo, Stanford University. (An abridged version is included in Moreitz and Landwehr, (1985), pp. 163–174.)

Bell, D. (1966), *The Reforming of General Education:the Columbia College Experience in its National Setting*, New York.

Bell, D. (1973), *The Coming of Post-Industrial Society*, New York.

BMFT (1984), *Bundesministerium für Forschung und Technologie, Informationstechnik*, Bonn.

BMFT (1985), *1984 und danach. Die gesellschaftliche Herausforderung der Informationstechnik*, mimeo (proceedings of an international conference).

BMFT/BMBW (1984), *Bundesministerium für Forschung und Technologie/Bundesministerium für Bildung und Wissenchaft, Computer und Bildung*, Bonn.

Bok, D. (1985), 'The President's report, 1983–84', *Harvard University Gazette*, 19 April.

Borbely, J. (1985), 'Changes in information technology: its implications for the graduate school curriculum', *Online*, March, pp. 126–8.

Bork, A. (1987), 'The potential for interactive technology', *Byte*, February, pp. 201–6.

Bronsema, G. S. and Keen, P. G. W. (1982), *Education and Implementation in MIS*, MIT, Center for Information Systems Research.

Clancey, W. J. (1986a), 'Qualitative student models', *Annual Review of Computer Science*, I, pp. 381–450.

Clancey, William J. (1986), 'Intelligent tutoring systems: a tutorial survey', in *Papers of the International Professorship in Computer Science (Expert Systems)*, Université de l'Etat, Namur, Belgium.

Clanchy, M. T. (1979), *From Memory to Written Record*, Cambridge, Mass.

Clapham, M. (1957), 'Printing', in Charles Singer et al. (eds), *A History of Technology*, Oxford, II.

Compaine, B. M. (1984), *Information Technology and Cultural Change: Toward a New Literacy?*, Program on Information Resources Policy, Harvard University.

Crichton, M. (1983), *Electronic Life. How to Think about Computers*, New York.

Education Turnkey Systems, Inc. (1985), *Uses of Computers in Education*, National Commission for Employment Policy (NCEP), Washington DC.

Eisenstein, E. (1979), *The Printing Press as an Agent of Change*, Cambridge University Press.

ETC (1984), Harvard Graduate School of Education, Educational Technology Center,

The Use of Information Technologies for Education in Science, Mathematics, and Computers. An Agenda for Research, mimeo.

Feigenbaum, E. A. and McCorduck, P. (1984), *The Fifth Generation: Artificial intelligence and Japan's Computer Challenge to the World*, rev. ed., New York.

Feurzieg, W. Horwitz, P. and Nickerson, R. S. (1981), *Microcomputers in Education*, Report for the Dept of HEW and NIE.

Fiske, E. B. (1984), 'Computers in the classroom', *New York Times*, 9, 10 and 11 December.

Forester, T. (ed.) (1981), *The Microelectronics Revolution*, Cambridge, Mass.

Gilmore, M. P. (1952), *The World of Humanism 1453–1517*, New York.

Von Gizycki, R. and Schubert, I. (1984), *Microelectronics: a Challenge for European Industrial Survival*, Munich.

Von Gizycki, R. and Weiler, U. (1980), *Mikroprozessoren und Bildungdwesen*, Munich.

Gottlieb Duttwiler Instituе (ed.) (forthcoming), *Computer Assisted Approaches to Training* (proceedings of a conference held in Lugano, Switzerland, on 25 and 26 May 1987; to be published by North Holland Publishing Co.).

Grafton, C. and Permaloff, A. (1984), 'Simulations and the microcomputer', *PS*, XVII, pp. 698–706.

Greenfield, P. (1984), *Mind and Media. The Effects of Television, Video Games and Computers*, Cambridge, Mass.

Haefner, K. (1982), *Die neue Bildungskrise*, Basel.

Hermeren, L. (1986), *The Departments of Linquistics and English at Brown. A Report on the Role of the Computer in Teaching and Research*, UHA, R and D Unit, Stockholm.

Hermeren, G. (1987), *Recent History of Computing at Brown University*, UHA, R and D Unit, Stockholm.

Jonscher, C. (1983), 'Information resources and economic productivity', *Information Economics and Policy*, I, pp. 13–35.

Keen, G. W. P. and Bronsema, G. S. (1982), *Strategic Computer Education*, MIT Center for Information Systems Research.

Kelsh, B. and Lindelow, J. (1982), 'Microcomputers in schools, promise and practice', *OSSC Bulletin*, 25 (B).

Kidder, T. (1982), *The Soul of a New Machine*, New York.

Landes, D. S. (1969), *The Unbound Prometheus*, Cambridge University Press.

Landes, D. S. (1983), *Revolution in Time: Clocks and the Making of the Modern World*, Cambridge, Mass.

Lehle, L. B. (1984), *Computers and Politics: a New Topic in Political Science*, paper delivered at the Annual Meeting of the APSA.

Lepper, M. R. and Malone T. W. (1987a), 'Intrinsic motivation and instructional effectiveness in computer-based education', in Snow, R. E. and Farr, M. J. (eds), *Aptitude, Learning, and Instruction: III. Conative and Affective Process Analysis*, Hillsdale, N. J.

Lepper, M. and Malone T. W. (1987b), 'Making learning fun: a taxonomy in intrinsic motivation learning', in Snow, R. E., and Farr, M. J. (eds) (') *Aptitude, Learning and Instruction: III Conative and Affective Process Analysis*, Hillsdale, N.J.

Lesgold, A. M. and Reif, F. (1983), *Computers in Education. Realising the Potential*, Washington DC.

Levien, R. (ed.), (1972), *The Emerging Technology. Instructional Usess of the Computer in Higher Education*, New York.

Levin, H. M. Glass G. V. and Meister, G. R. (1984), *Cost-Effectiveness of Four Educational Interventions*, Stanford University, Institute for Research on Educational Finance and Governance (IFG).

Linelow, J. (1983), *Administrator's Guide to Computers in the Classroom*, Eugene, Oregon: ERIC.

Meeks, B. N. (1987), 'The quiet revolution. On-line education becomes a real alternative', *Byte*, February pp. 183–90.

MIT (1984a), *Project ATHENA, Faculty/Studen Projects*, mimeo.

MIT (1984b), *Status Report on Project ATHENA*, mimeo.

MIT (1984c), *Management in the Nineties*. A research proposal by the Sloan Shool of Management, mimeo.

Miura I. T. and Hess, R. (1984), *Issues in Training Teachers to Use Microcomputers in the Classroom: Examples from the United States*, Stanford University, IFG.

Moreitz, M. and Landwehr, R. (eds), (1985), *Der Sprung in die Zukunft. Zur Bedeutung der Informations – und Kommunikationstechnologien für soziale Entwicklung*, Weinheim.

Naiman, A. (1987), 'A hard look at educational software', *Byte*, February, pp. 193–200.

Noble D. (1984), 'The underside of computer literacy', *Raritan, III*, pp. 37–64.

Oettinger A. G. (1969), *Run, Computer, Run*, Cambridge, Mass.

Oettinger A. G. (1984), *The Compunications Age*, Harvard University, Program on Information Resources Policy, mimeo.

Office of Technology Assessment (OTA) (1983), *International Competitiveness in Electronics*, Washington DC.

Olds, H. F. Schwartz J. L. and Willie, N. (1980), *People and Computers: Who Teaches Whom?*, Newton, Mass Education Development Center, Inc., mimeo.

Osgood, D. (1987), 'The difference in higher education', *Byte*, February, pp. 165–78.

Pogrow, S. (1983), *Education in the Computer Age. Issues of Policy, Practice, and Reform*, Beverly Hills/London.

Pollock, F. (1956), *Automation. Risiko und Chance*, Frankfurt (American edition 1957, New York).

Pepe, J. et al. (1984), *Microcomputers in Schools, 1983–84*, Market Data, Westport, CT.

Quillard, J. A. et al. (1983), *A Study of the Corporate Use of Personal Computers*, MIT, Center for Information Systems Research.

Rockart, J. F. and Scott Morton, M. S. (1975), *Computers and the Learning Process in Higher Education*, New York.

'Revolution im Unterricht: Computer wird Pflicht', *Der Spiegel*, 47/1984, pp. 97–129.

Schmidt, P. (1985), 'The computer as tutor', *New York Times Education Survey*, 14 April.

Schumann, G. (1984), 'The macro- and microeconomic social impact of advanced computer technology', *Futures*, June, pp. 260–85.

Senator, S. Trinity F. and Roper, W. (1984), *Computers in the Classroom: A Program for New Jersey*, Princeton University, Woodrow Wilson School for Public and International Affairs.

Shavelson R. J. et al. (1983), *Teachers' Instructional Uses of Microcomputers*, Rand Paper, Santa Monica, CA.

Sheingold, K. Kane, J. H. and Endreweit, M. E. (1983), 'Microcomputer use in schools: developing a research agenda', *Harvard Educational Review, 53*, November, pp. 412–32.

Suppes, P. (1966), 'The uses of computers in education', *Scientific American*, September, pp. 207–20.

Svenning, C. (1987), *Computing Social Reality. A case Study of an American Computer-Intensive University*, Stockholm: UHA, R and D Unit.

Van Treeck, W. (1985), *Programmieren durch Sachbearbeiter und Facharbeiter*, mimeo, University of Kassel.

Turkle, S. (1984), *The Second Self*, New York.

Axler Turner, J. (1985), 'Multimillion-dollar projects to study uses of Computers suffer setbacks on three campuses', *Chronicle of Higher Education*, 5 June, pp. 15–16.

Axler Turner, J. (1986a), 'Carnegie Mellon unveils "Andrew" a computing system for colleges', *Chronicle of Higher Education*, 29 January, p. 20.

Axler Turner, J. (1986), 'At Clarkson U., every student has a "Z", but computer "Geeks" are few', *Chronicle of Higher Education*, 10 December, pp. 1, 30, 31.

Axler Turner, J. (1987), 'Drive to require students to buy computers slows', *Chronicle of Higher Education*, 4 February, pp. 1, 28.

US House of Representatives (1983), *Computers and Education*, Hearings Before the Sub-Committee on Investigations and Oversight of the Committee on Science and Technology, 28 and 29 September.

Wheeler, D. L. (1987), 'Artificial-intelligence researchers develop electronic "Tutors" to aid learning process', *Chronicle of Higher Education*, 20 May, pp. 6–8.

White, D. and Rampy, L. (1983), *Solutions Unlimited: Delphi Study on Policy Issues in the Introduction and Management of Computers in Classroom*, in Agency for Instructional Television, mimeo, Bloomington.

Mapping the social sciences: the contribution of technology to information retrieval

EUGENE GARFIELD *ISI (USA)*
ROBERT KIMBERLEY *ISI (UK)*
DAVID A. PENDLEBURY *ISI (USA)*

INTRODUCTION

By virtue of the computer's storage capacity, its powers of speed and specificity in retrieval and, above all, its economy, technology has reshaped knowledge classification.

At least since the time of Plato and Aristotle – even before their era if we wish to consider mythographers – humans have been ardent classificationists. It is obvious, however, that human subjective judgement produces taxonomies that partially reflect objective reality and partially the mind of the taxonomer. John H. Finley Jr, in writing about how the early Greeks ordered their world, observed that 'thought proceeds by scheme and sequence; it manipulates, puts things where it wants them, makes different designs from any that the eyes see'. (Finley, 1966, p. 8). Human classification schemes, such as subject heading categories, are, then, inherently subjective, owing to the perceptions upon which they are based.

The alternative is an objective or natural system of classification in which the attributes of objects (their similarities or differences) are the defining elements. Such a system of classification, while theoretically possible, was not a practical pursuit without computer technology.

It is assuredly not the aim of this chapter to describe the manifold ways in which information technology (IT) is being exploited today to aid researchers in the social and behavioural sciences. Nor do we intend to comment on how this IT has changed the nature and type of research projects undertaken by social scientists. (It is plain, however, that quantification has been a hallmark of the social sciences since the

Second World War. And it is no coincidence that researchers became increasingly interested in quantitative studies at the same time that the introduction of computers made such activities feasible.) Rather, this chapter focuses on the efforts of the Institute for Scientific Information (ISI), a producer of computer-based information products for researchers in the sciences, social sciences, and humanities, to create a natural system of classifying knowledge (or more narrowly, research activity) through the use of citation indexing and, more recently, 'geographic' maps of research through co-citation clustering.

CITATION INDEXING

E. Garfield applied the principle of citation indexing to the academic literature (Garfield, 1979). Citation indexing was first used in *Shepard's Citations*, an index for the legal profession to precedents of the Federal and State courts. In drawing an analogy between the progression of legal decisions based on precedents, and scientific research based on previously published results, Garfield imagined the utility of citation indexing in the scientific literature (Garfield, 1955).

The principle underlying citation indexing is as follows: if one paper cites an earlier publication, they bear a conceptual relationship to one another. The references given in a publication thus serve to link that publication to earlier knowledge. Implicit in these linkages is a relatedness of intellectual content. In reordering the literature by works cited, we obtain a citation index. Citation indexing is a natural or automatic system of classification: the material to be classified orders itself through its conceptual links (Garfield, Malin and Small, 1975).

After succeeding in developing a citation index to the scientific literature – the *Science Citation Index (SCI)* – Garfield applied the technique to the literature of the social sciences (Garfield, 1964). Since 1966 ISI has published the *Social Sciences Citation Index (SSCI)*. In 1985 the *SSCI* fully covered about 1,500 journals and selectively covered some 3,300 more, for a total of about 4,800 journals representing over twenty-five different fields. In 1985 alone over 120,000 articles, reviews, letters, editorials, abstracts, etc., and nearly 1.5 million references from these items were indexed. The *SSCI* has become an important tool for researchers in the social sciences. Since a citation index gives access not only to the publications indexed, but also to cited works, the *SSCI* is multidisciplinary in scope. Moreover, the user of a citation index is not limited to retrospective searching. The *SSCI* reveals what current publications have cited an older work.